PROMOTE 'EM LIKE ROCKSTAR!
A Track Parent's Essential Guide to Hacking the Athletic Recruitment Process
and Soaring from Nada to Bada-BOOM
in 30 days or Less

CARA D. JACKSON

Disclaimer

in this eBook, you are taking full responsibility for your actions.

Acknowledgements

This book is dedicated to all track parents. It's for those who arrive for the field events and don't leave until the 4X400m relay. It's especially for mothers, who have tirelessly watched, cheered for, and supported their kids year after year, through the hot summer months, long after school track season is over. It's for fathers who sit in the stands timing splits on relays as well as others who transport pole vault sticks from track to track on top of their vehicle.

This book is for parents, like me, who see the talent and desire that our children possess and want to help them pursue athletics at the next level. It is for anyone who refuses to sit back and accept whatever happens to fall in their lap, but instead teaches their kids to go after what they want with specific, unrelenting, and fearless action.

This is for my children, especially my daughter, whose path gave me a story to tell and an experience to share.

With special thanks to my husband and trackmate for his encouragement, friendship and support in all that I do.

Contents

HOW TO GET THE MOST OUT OF THIS TRACK RECRUITING BOOK

Before you get started, there are a few important steps that you should do to make this learning experience interactive and to maximize your benefit from this guide.

1. **Use the Promote 'Em Like a Rockstar Workbook** to jot down notes and to systematically complete each step. The workbook will help keep you organized, plus it will make it easy for you to quickly access essential information in a time crunch.

2. **Pay special attention to the "Tips"** that are listed throughout the chapters of the book. These tidbits often give key information that will help you along in this process. Some offer advice or instructions, while others share opportunities that are available to student-athletes with special circumstances.

3. **Click on the links.** You will notice that I've included links to different track related websites that are important for the informed athlete and their parents to access throughout the recruitment process. In certain cases, I have an affiliate relationship with the sites, so if you choose to use their services, when registering, please use the code "Cara Jackson" to inform them that you heard about them from me.

4. If you like the idea of promoting your athlete but need a little more assistance with the process, I can help. Just shoot me an email, and we can talk about your best options and how I can guide you through this process.

mytrackrockstar@gmail.com

5. **Let me know how you feel**. I have done my best to cover as much information in a concise and easily understandable way. If you like it, let me know. If there is something that you wish I would have covered, but did not, let me know by shooting me an email. Hopefully, I've earned your 5-star review.

6. **Join my mailing list**. If you are hungry for more, please take advantage of my FREE monthly track recruitment updates.

I hope you enjoy joining me on this journey and wish you much success in achieving the ultimate goal of getting your athlete recruited!

INTRODUCTION

Don't Gamble with Your Rockstar's Future

You're the parent of a promising high school track athlete. You know they have the skill and discipline to run at the next level. You've had them under great coaches, watched their times and marks improve, and they even have a bucket full of medals in the corner of their bedroom as proof of their track greatness. Now they say they want to compete in college. You're excited and on board with the potential because a track scholarship would be a great help in covering their college expenses.

But where are the recruitment calls?

Your athlete is looking at you, you're looking to their coaches, and still there are no calls coming in from colleges.

You want to do more, but you're feeling frustrated. You've scoured the internet, but the information online is all very confusing, the recruitment terminology is foreign, and to make matters worse, time is dwindling.

So now what?

Believe it or not, for most track athletes, even the ones who are at the top of their athletic game, college recruitment does not just happen because you've been on the field, track or in the pit. Sadly, despite the time, money and energy dedicated in preparation and competition, many high school students, parents and even coaches have no idea how to translate high school athletics into college recruitment.

Sound familiar? If so, I'm here to tell you there's a proven way to get your athlete on the radar of college coaches, and it's easy to learn!

Humor me for a moment and think of your athlete as a product, let's say a movie.

Sounds crazy? Just let me continue.

Have you ever noticed that when a new movie is released, trailers show up on the internet, top-rated Hollywood stars appear on late night and daytime talk shows, eye-catching billboards pop up along the interstate, and sometimes zany character toys are dropped into your kids' nuggets meal, all in an effort to promote the movie? Months, sometimes even years, before the movie is released we begin hearing about and anticipating the upcoming release date. If you're anything like my kids, you've not only watched the trailers repeatedly, but you're already making plans for the premier showing.

Well, this is proof that even after spending millions of dollars to produce it and casting A-List actors, these movies can easily go unheard of without proper advertising and promotions. In Hollywood, nothing is left to chance, and your child's athletic career is no different. While you may not have invested millions, you have made a serious financial and time investment (in your standards) in your child's success that should be treated no differently than a Hollywood blockbuster. This is a true and undeniable fact. No, I'm not suggesting that you post your kid's face on the highway billboard, but please understand that it takes preparation, planning and promotion to get on the athletic recruitment radar. It is up to you to work as your child's advocate and marketing specialist to make this happen.

Like I mentioned earlier, you are your child's Don King or Sharon Osborne, if you will. That's right, it's up to you. What I'm saying is that you are their promoter. Remember, Beyoncé does the singing, but the promoter arranges the gigs. With this in mind, it's your responsibility to not only position them to achieve their athletic goals, but to inform all the right people when they do so. Hold on, I know what you're thinking...my school coach is very dedicated to his/her athletes and they told me they would guide my child through this process or I'm paying his/her AAU Coach to do this so that I don't have to. If that's the case, I'm not gonna knock it, but I do encourage you to read on.

Now let's think logically about this for a moment.

Many high school coaches, even those with the best intentions, have track team rosters among some of the highest in sports participation in the school. Now for the kicker...some of them are not only coaching the boys track team, but the girls as well. Understanding that, it is easy to see that their time is limited. Managing classroom responsibilities, because most high school coaches are teachers, compounded by team training, travel and organizing competitions, not to mention the demands of their personal lives outside of school duties, their hands are full. For a select few athletes, they may go above and beyond to assist, but it is unreasonable, risky, unfair and unrealistic to expect that your child's school coach will be able to dedicate the necessary time to assist each athlete with creating a personalized recruitment plan, maintain ongoing and regular communication and even have the vision and knowledge to meet your child's specific school desires and needs.

Seems a bit risky, don't you think?

Are you really willing to drop all the hopes and dreams of your family on this coach's lap?

I think not!

To be perfectly honest, I understand that your hesitancy may come from inexperience. You may lack confidence in this area because you've never done this before. Maybe you're up at night worrying about how your child will pay for college and if all this running will amount to more than just fun competition against rival schools. Or, maybe you never played a college sport or attended college at all, for that matter. Well consider this, you never walked until you learned either, and this is no different.

Obviously, you picked up this book for some reason, so that tells me that you realize there is a need or void in this process. Well, I'm here to tell you that you can change all of that. In fact, you owe it to yourself and your athlete to pull up a chair to your computer, take out your cell phone or wherever you work best, and get ready to take notes. It's time to commit to learning this process.

As we go through this journey together, just remember, you don't have to be perfect, nor does your athlete. In fact, from here on out, we're going to refer to your athlete as a Rockstar, because that's how you're going to promote 'em.

Now, let's take a step back.

Before you read any further, take a deep breath and just relax. I know you may be feeling under the gun that time is slipping through your fingers, stressed or pressured in some way. Maybe you're frustrated that no college coaches have called or emailed. You may be thinking about the Time Energy & Dollars (TEDS) that you've invested and wondering if it was a waste.

Or maybe it's something else.

Regardless of your starting point, you've come to the right resource. The information shared in this book will teach you to be your own advocate and to promote your athlete like a Rock Star.

Can you afford not to?

In the next few hours or weeks (however long it takes you to read this book), you're going to learn a step-by-step way of promoting your track athlete and succeeding in the recruitment game. Yes, this information will put you in the driver's seat. And I know, it's a big mental tweak, but the results are going to be so simple and effective you're going to kick yourself for not reading this sooner.

WHO AM I AND WHY SHOULD YOU LISTEN TO ME?

"If you want to be successful,
find someone who has achieved the results you want
and copy what they do, and you'll achieve the same results."
Tony Robbins

Some years ago, when my daughter reached high school, I began researching how athletes get recruited. Initially, like most parents, I thought making the times, distances or marks would be enough. Over time, I discovered something different. Many parents, who after doling out cash for club teams, spending 3-day weekends cheering in the hot sun, and paying top dollar for swanky uniforms have no idea how their child will be recruited to run track in college. Then I discovered something else. Many high school coaches don't know either.

That breakthrough led me down a path of further exploration. I began reading book after book, researching countless websites, attending seminars and asking questions of collegiate coaches and other informed people about athletic recruitment. What I learned armed me with the tools to help my daughter get recruited as a track athlete and commit at the beginning of her senior year. Throughout the process, I recorded all our steps to create a blueprint to use with my other children.

Many friends and other track parents became excited and curious. That's when the calls started, and they began pulling me aside at track meets to find out how we did it. Realizing that I was in a position to empower other parents with information and tools to impact their runner's future, I decided to write this book. I recognized that the same way I helped my daughter, other parents can follow a few simple steps as laid out in these pages, to do the same.

Why would others want to know what I did?

Like you, I was a track parent. With five kids draining on my pockets, basically stair-steps in age, I knew they would need a superior skill or talent that could help cover the ever-increasing expenses of college tuition. Equally important, my husband and I wanted to invest their time in something fun and rewarding. So, we looked for an activity that had multiple benefits, and could possibly be a way to pay for college.

Well, we both ran in high school and my husband continued at the collegiate level. We later began to run in road races as adults, while pushing the kids in a stroller. That's how my kids were first introduced to and eventually became excited about running. Naturally, track became the go to activity.

Skipping ahead a few years, we made the decision to start training our own summer track team. This opened the doors for us to meet and build relationships with other professionals in the field. It also triggered the need to educate ourselves in the sport and mattes related to it.

What is so special about this information?

I'll be the first to admit that there's a ton of valuable information that's easily accessible from the internet. In fact, there are pages upon pages of stuff. That's partially how I learned. However, it takes a lot of time to go through all of it to figure out what you can use and what's not important. Plus, most of it is for athletes in general (not just track), and particularly football players. By following this plan that I am giving you, will allow you to cut to the chase, plus it's specific to track athletes. In your hands, you have the tools to jumpstart the recruitment process. Since I've already laid the groundwork, you'll be ahead of where I started, because I'm going to share with you what I learned and how I've applied that knowledge.

How do you get your athlete recruited?

Most don't have a clue. It doesn't just happen because your child is talented and there generally isn't someone out there waiting to help your family through this process for free. It will take work, you'll have to apply the information as instructed, and you'll have to stay organized. It's simple, but not necessarily easy.

Depending on the grade of your athlete, you may not be able to just sit down and read straight through this book. There's a lot of valuable information, but if you're in a time crunch, you may need to jump around to get right down to the nitty gritty. If that is your situation, pay special attention to the "Step" labeled chapters. That'll be your shortcut, but you can always go back to pick up other essential details as needed.

It's also important to realize that all high school sports have their unique aspects of recruitment, and track and field is no different. In fact, most athletic recruitment information is written for football players with hopes that some elements can be applied to track. Truth is, one of the biggest differences with track and football is that track and field is an equivalency sport. Unlike football, basketball and a few other sports which in many cases provide full ride scholarships to all athletes, equivalency sports divide scholarship dollars among athletes. This doesn't mean that your Rockstar cannot get his or her full college expenses covered. It just means you'll have to pay more attention to details and work this plan that I will share with you.

Why hasn't my athlete been recruited?

Many parents ask this of themselves all the time (especially when senior year track season rolls around) and with good reason. You've invested TEDs (as a I once heard it called) to prepare your athlete, they've earned respectable marks, and they have the desire to continue running. So, why haven't they been contacted by a college coach yet?

The Six Elements

Usually the blue-chip prospects who rank at the top of the recruitment list have no problems getting early and direct communication from coaches, maybe even home visits. A few other athletes are able to benefit from the assistance of their school coach, but in most cases, opportunities are sought out by parents who are prepared, persistent and sometimes bossy. These parents have truly accepted that their parenting job is not over. They stay informed on their kids academic and athletic performance and do not leave anything to chance. They follow a basic plan that incorporates the same elements that I will share with you in the upcoming pages of this book. These six elements are simple but completing them will require effort and patience.

#1 make the grades

#2 make the times, distances or heights

#3 make the effort to understand your options (get informed)

#4 make the impression

#5 make the visit

#6 make the decision

In Promote 'em Like a Rockstar, I've laid out the steps in an easily understandable way. All you have to do is apply what you read to maximize your results. Anyone who desires to help an athlete can apply the information in this book. Although most of it is written to the parent, it is equally important for your student-athlete to read and take an active role in this process. Hopefully, you will follow the plan and stick to it, to help your Rockstar get recruited. Now it's up to you to make it happen.

MYTHS ATHLETE'S BELIEVE ABOUT RECRUITMENT

"If you don't go after what you want, you'll never have it. If you don't ask, the answer is always no. If you don't step forward, you're always in the same place."
Nora Roberts

Dear Athlete,

It's your senior year, you've won county, you were voted captain and selected team MVP, and maybe even made it to the podium in your state championship meet, so why isn't your phone bombarded with calls from college coaches?

After all, you've dedicated 15+ hours each week to training and competitions, kept your grades in order and even took the SAT and ACT exams to see where you would score highest. Is it wrong to expect something in return?

Well, this is the unfortunate reality for many athletes across the nation, who in fact have the potential to compete at the next level but may have been misinformed or have fallen prey to one or more myths of athletic recruitment.

Before you dive in head first, let's take an honest look at a few of the myths that you may falsely believe, and as a result are holding you back...

Myths:

#1 If I do the work, colleges will find me.

#2 My high school coach will get me into school.

#3 If coaches don't call it is because they do not need me.

#4 I haven't participated in my senior year state championship meet yet, and that is when this process really gets started.

#5 It's better to let someone else do it, because what if I fail?

Do any of these sound familiar? I can promise you that you aren't the only one who can answer yes to at least one of these false beliefs. And I don't mind admitting to you that I was once in the same boat.

Now let's debunk these myths...

#1 If I do the work, colleges will find me...no siree, unless you're ranked in the top 20 in the nation this is probably not the case. If you're like most, you have hit some competitive times or marks that could easily go unnoticed if you don't speak up. Remember, the squeaky wheel gets the oil.

#2 My high school coach will get me into school...wrong again! Obviously, there are coaches who have relationships with college teams, but chances are they only have a handful of them. What's the likelihood that one of those schools is actually one you are interested in and that it has an opening for an athlete in your event during your graduation year? While your coach can provide great support and maybe a wonderful recommendation letter, it's not fair to expect them to cater to yours and your teammates' individual needs throughout the recruitment process. Trust me, this is a time where you need to take matters into your own hands.

#3 If coaches don't call it is because they do not need me...Just like myth #1, you may have just slipped under their radar or maybe your marks are borderline. Either way, you'll never know if you're needed if you don't reach out to let them know you're interested.

#4 I haven't participated in my senior year state championship meet yet, and that is when this process really gets started...if you believe that, thank goodness you're reading this book. You'll be surprised to learn that track is about times, heights and distances, not age and grade. You can get on a coach's radar as early as ninth grade, even middle school if your times are competitive enough.

#5 It's better to let someone else do it, because what if I fail?...By reading this, you've taken the first step, which probably means you're already ahead of 90% of your counterparts. Plus, this is really a numbers game which makes it virtually fail-proof. The more closely you follow the steps shared in this book, the greater your chances of success. In most cases, there is typically a school somewhere that can use an athlete with your skills.

Myths debunked. Let's move forward. Capiche?

No matter where you are in your recruitment process, I guarantee that the information in this book will result in more positive changes than anything else you've done leading up to now.

You'll also be glad to know that because your success is so important to me, and I already think of you as a Rockstar, I'll do my best to keep you awake and motivated while flipping these pages.

Okay, what now?

It's   your   move.

CHAPTER 1

WHY SOME ATHLETES ALWAYS WIN BIG, AND OTHERS STRUGGLE FOREVER

"By failing to prepare, you are preparing to fail."
Benjamin Franklin

Let's talk about how to put yourself in a better position to be recruited.

I've been a longtime fan of track and field, an athlete, and a coach. It's been my observation that there are some fairly consistent reasons why some athletes absolutely ignite the track and others just consistently seem to produce too little too late.

Let me share a story to express my point.

Our boys high school soccer program is fun to watch, but we do not have a strong history of sending athletes to college. It's more of a "fun" experience that allows students to build great memories and be a part of a team. Well, my son overheard a conversation in class where one of the soccer players was asked what he was doing to improve his skills. The athlete quickly responded, "we practice as a team and on our own we get together and kick the ball around on the upper field." The other student looked at him, and replied, "No, I'm asking about

1

what you're doing to improve your skill level- like drills, agility training, speed work." The soccer player's voice cracked with annoyance, as he retorted, "it doesn't work like that in soccer!" Without hesitation, the other student responded, "what you're doing is the same thing every other soccer player from our school has done in the past, and if you keep that up you'll get the same result."

Powerful! What was just described epitomizes the true yet cliché definition of insanity - doing the same thing over and over and expecting different results.

While there is no hard-and-fast rule to winning big, and of course there are some factors such as skill, gene-pool and heart that will impact your Rockstar's success, there are also recognizable patterns that most successful track athletes have followed. One of the most valuable factors is how you spend your summer.

6 Catastrophic Summer Choices that Can Derail Your Recruitment Plan

Catastrophic Choice #1: <u>Not training with a skilled coach</u>
Just like the soccer boys who kicked the ball around, it's not enough for your Rockstar to train without a plan. To get the best results you need to choose an AAU / USATF registered track and field team. Most programs work with kids from ages 8-18 years old. You can easily google AAU or USATF and your city to find a local team.

Many of these coaches are experienced runners and former collegiate track athletes themselves. They understand what it takes to get to the next level and are dedicated to equipping each young athlete with these tools. Some have trained Olympians.

http://www.usatf.org

http://aautrackandfield.org

Catastrophic Choice #2: Not attending a sports camp
The summers of freshman and sophomore years are great times to participate in track camps and clinics on college campuses. The university's coaching staff typically hosts these camps right at the stadium or facility where the actual school athletes train. You might even find a handful of student-athletes present during these camps. This is a great way to get in front of a coach to show them more than your stats.

Be advised, track camps can be a bit pricey. The average cost is about $450, which equates to anywhere from $100-$125 per day, give or take. If you are considering this option, just know that camps are money-making opportunities for universities, so not all programs are equal.

Important factors in selecting a camp:

3

- <u>Always investigate the athlete-to-coach ratio</u> - too many kids can translate to too little attention for your Rockstar

- <u>Age range of participants</u> - you want a group in your age range. In most cases coaches tend to focus on the older kids who are closer to graduation, which may or may not work in your favor.

- <u>Are students separated based on skill level</u> - Don't waste time mixed into a group of beginners. You won't get the attention or benefit from being in this environment.

Like I said, this is not required, but if it is within your budget, staying overnight at a track camp may be a good way for your Rockstar to truly get to know a school and its coaching staff. A camp could put your Rockstar in a position to add or deduct a university from their Target list.

Here are links to two camp resources:

Lists Track & XC Camps across the nation on Milesplit
http://camps.milesplit.com/

Complete Track & Field Summer Clinic for High School Athletes (hosted at Harvard University)
https://completetrackandfield.com/clinic/

Catastrophic Choice #3: <u>Not competing in track meets with stiff competition</u>

It's not enough to just train, athletes must compete. While there is some wiggle room for the longer distances, because many are following their cross-country summer training plan, this is especially true for sprinters, hurdlers and jumpers. Competition breeds faster runners. Just watch Milesplit times drop as the summer season progresses. If you're not out there, you're liable to get left in the dust. Plus, with these track meets being in other states and regions, you're no longer confined to competing against the same county or in-state teams that you saw all school year. Greater competition forces athletes to raise the bar on what they are willing to give.

Another important benefit is gaining yet another opportunity to improve your times. Waiting a whole year after the school season ends could be a disastrous move.

<u>http://www.milesplit.com/rankings/leaders/high-school-boys/outdoor-track-and-field</u>

Catastrophic Choice #4: <u>Not establishing a profile that gives coaches a clear picture</u>

In high school track the top two athletes compete. If you're #3 or higher, this can pose a serious problem. If you don't run the events, you don't have times on your profile. However, just because you're not within the top two athletes on your respective team, doesn't mean that you aren't running at scholarship level. Bottomline, coaches can't recruit an athlete

5

with no times. The good news is, with summer track, there is no limit to the number of athletes on a team who can participate in an event. In fact, every single athlete can participate in the 200m race, for instance, if they so desire.

By competing over the summer you're able to strategically develop your profile and fill in any gaps about your abilities that may be present in your school profile alone.

Catastrophic Choice #5: <u>Not dedicating time to standardized test preparation</u>

Don't let a poor SAT score keep your Rockstar from getting ahead. Let's face it, these exams can spell the difference between failure or success when it comes to the college application. Our Rockstars must realize that it is truly academics first when it comes to track and field. I've witnessed less talented athletes earn greater opportunities because of their performance in the classroom. At the same time, I've seen elite runners end up a day late and a dollar short because their grades were too low.

When it comes to standardized testing:

- It is necessary to take at least one of these exams in order to be accepted into most institutions – SAT or ACT.

- The ACT composite score is key

- First test should be taken no later than sophomore year

- Retake, retake, retake. Try to change your study format between retakes.

- You must prepare. There are many options for the busy student-athlete:

  - self-paced sites like Khan Academy or PrepScholar

  - using a hard copy of an official test prep guide

  - attend a test prep class led by a professional tutor (group or individualized)

  - A combination of the above options

I truly recommend using a classroom environment for test prep at least one time. Something this important is not worth the gamble. If necessary, your Rockstar can pick up a babysitting job to earn the money to pay halfsies on it. It's just that important.

Trust me, when it comes to registering for the exam, the process will take much longer than you think, so don't wait until the eleventh hour to get started.

My daughter used Prep Scholars' self-paced program, which I would recommend to any athlete with a busy schedule. They offer other options to meet the needs of any student athlete. If you choose to use PrepScholar, please include "Cara Jackson" as the referral source:

(Click below if you want to get SAT & ACT help)

https://www.prepscholar.com/

> **Tip:** 11th & 12th grade students who receive free lunch may be eligible to receive a standardized test fee waiver. Check with your counselor for details on how this is handled at your high school.

Catastrophic Choice #6: Overestimating What You Are Doing to Prepare

Sports are competitions where not everyone will win. Don't let your Rockstar get caught up thinking that running unbridled mileage is going to get them the end goal, just because they're doing something. If you're working, others are too. Trust me, athletes are working smart and following a plan. If they're not doing what the top athletes are doing, the result won't be pretty. It takes work to be a collegiate athlete, and that's just a fact. If you're ready to train like a champion, scroll down and find the link to access a proven training plan for your event:

Sprinters
Marc Mangiacotti - Complete 100 Meter Development

Latif Thomas - Complete HS 400 Meter Training

Marc Mangiacotti - Advanced Concepts in Training 400 Meter Runners

Complete Speed Training 2

Middle Distance
Scott Christensen - Complete Middle Distance (800-1600)

Ron Grigg - Complete Program Design for 400/600/800 Meter Runners

Hurdlers
Tony Veney - Advanced Sprint (100/110) Hurdle Development

Field Events
Boo Schexnayder - Complete Technique & Teaching for the Jumping Events

Cross Country
Scott Christensen - Complete HS Cross Country Training

Complete Track & Field Products:
http://www.completetrackandfield.com/cmd.php?af=168605
4

CHAPTER 2

SETTING THE STAGE

*"Opportunity does not waste time with those who are
unprepared"*
Idowu Koyenikan

When it comes to getting recruited to play a sport in college,
like almost everything, it is about being prepared, not luck. In
order to prepare, one must take action.

Before your Rockstar can begin the recruitment process, there
are some important elements that must be in place. Without
these, no matter how talented of a thrower or sprinter your
Rockstar may be, they will not be eligible for consideration if
they fail to meet these minimum standards:

1. **Take the required Core Classes.** Currently, there are 16
   required classes as determined by the NCAA. These core
   classes include a combination of English, math,
   natural/physical science, social science, foreign language,
   comparative religion or philosophy. Be advised, the
   academic standards may vary based on the division level,
   so it is important that you check the NCAA link and speak
   with your school counselor to ensure that you are taking
   the appropriate classes. With these core classes, an athlete
   will also be eligible to compete at the NAIA and NJCAA

levels. A few examples of classes that may be required or offered by your school but <u>do not</u> count towards your core classes include: Health, Physical Education, Drama, Music, and Art

2. **Make the grades.** The two biggest differentiators that determine at what level athletes will compete are athleticism and grades. Your Rockstar must accept that he has control over his grades. It is really a matter of mindset, time and effort. They must find a way to get the grades, and not just the minimum, but to excel. Seek out resources within your school or tutors outside of your school if your Rockstar finds himself having difficulty with classes. There's even Khan Academy for most subjects if you have internet access. If you don't know where to start, schedule a meeting with their school counselor. Most counselors have a wealth of information that may not be widely publicized. For some students, these services are free. Get the help your Rockstar needs while you still have a chance to make a difference.

3. **Meeting a minimum score on the standardized testing: ACT or SAT.** It is important to know the NCAA minimum standards listed below:

ACT – 16 SAT – 860

Again, I want to really hit home that the goal is not to just meet the minimum standard, but to exceed. Your Rockstar's scores translate to money when it comes to

11

college admissions, so these exams are a serious matter. Merely shooting for these minimum standards will undoubtedly put you outside of the mark for many schools. However, Division I athletics offers some leniency by using a sliding scale that compares GPA to test scores. What this means is that in some cases, a low test score can be compensated by a high grade point average, and vice versa. Again, you'll need to speak with your counselor and check the NCAA or NAIA websites for specifics.

4. **Train to perform your best** - Hit your best times and marks to meet the scholarship standard preferably by the end of summer following Junior year at the latest. Playing a sport in college is a privilege that is not accessible to everyone. The only thing that truly sets your Rockstar apart from the average collegiate intramural athlete is their ability to meet the scholarship standard. Many of them love the sport, may dedicate countless hours to preparation and may have even been playing the sport longer. So, it is imperative that your Rockstar meets the scholarship standard early enough to take advantage of the recruitment process, if they want to be considered in this select group of student-athletes.

5. **Building relationships with the right people.** As they say, "birds of a feather flock together." Friends, associates and even teammates should be moving in a similar direction as your Rockstar. Really, one of the best aspects of playing sports in high school and college is being with like-minded people. Similarly, relationships with people

who are in a position to guide, assist and write recommendations is also important. Student-athletes should feel comfortable sitting down and talking with the school counselor and coach about future college plans. They need to know who your Rockstar is and not just their name. Many recommendations are requested senior year, and in most cases student-athletes nor parents are privy to what is said or written. Armed with a pen, these people can open and close doors that you didn't even know existed. It's also important to represent yourself in competitions well, because some student-athletes may need to rely on a competitor's coach to speak kind words on their behalf.

CHAPTER 3

THE PARENT'S ROLE IN THE RECRUITMENT PROCESS

*"Behind every young child who believes in himself
is a parent who believed first."*
The Fresh Quotes

The fact that you're still reading this book, there's no doubt about it, we share similar concerns for our child(ren) and their future success (both professionally and financially). We both have invested a lot of TEDS which has resulted in a possible future for our athletes in collegiate sports. So, remember, I found a light at the end of the tunnel, and if you follow my plan you can too.

But first, you need to realize that you are no longer just a parent spectator - but the Manager of a Rock Star athlete. In fact, I'm going to teach you to not just be your Rockstar's greatest cheerleader, but their very own Don King. You will publicize, advertise and make a match with as many coaches as possible, which in turn, will result in money for college.

Before we do anything, we must first set the stage. What I mean is that certain tasks need to be in order before we can get this ball rolling. With that said, it is your responsibility as

Manager to follow the first step in the Promote 'Em Like a Rockstar Plan, which is to prepare for success by keeping things in order.

While your Rockstar is training and putting in time on the track, the manager should put together the following system to organize all communication:

STEP 1: SET UP A SYSTEM TO ORGANIZE YOUR DATA

- <u>Create a Unique Email account using Gmail which is strictly for the Rockstar Plan</u>. You will be emailing many coaches and receiving responses that you don't want to miss. Don't take the chance of messages getting mixed in with your personal stuff. You also don't want to risk messages going to your Rockstar's account, which could go undetected and unopened because they don't check their messages often enough. Both parent and Rockstar should have access to this Gmail account.

Here's a good name:

firstnamelastnamegradyear@gmail.com
(keep it simple and professional)

Ex: JonDoe2019@gmail.com

- <u>Use Google Drive to manage all your data</u>. If you don't know how to use Google Drive, now is the time to learn.

15

If you know Microsoft Office than learning this should be a snap. These tools are almost identical, Google Drive just has fewer capabilities.

Here are some items that you will create:
- Target school database
- Email template for coaches
- One-page Athletic Profile

The best things I've found about working in Google Drive is that you can easily access it anywhere and it automatically saves your work, so you don't have to worry about losing anything.

- <u>Attach your Gmail account to your phone</u> so that you will be able to respond to messages timely
- <u>Get a notebook</u> to record handwritten notes from coaches' calls
- <u>Scan data into your computer</u>: ACT Results, Unofficial Transcripts, List of Senior year classes) -get a copy of each from your school's counseling office
- <u>Get Your NCAA Number</u>

Most of these steps are self-explanatory, but I will go into further detail regarding the NCAA number.

Getting Your NCAA Number

Let's get ready to REGISTER!!! As they say, "creating an account with the NCAA (or NAIA) Eligibility Center is your first step to becoming a student-athlete."

Here's what you'll need to know. The NCAA is the largest of two governing bodies over college athletics. The other is the NAIA. We'll touch more on the details of these entities in the next chapter, because for now our focus is on registering with the eligibility centers. The NCAA sets the rules and regulations for what, when and how colleges and student-athletes can interact. They work behind the scenes to support college athletes. Some of these areas include: academic endeavors, access to services such as health insurance, funding for NCAA championship meets, and help in emergency situations, such as money for a flight home, winter gear, or a laptop, just to name a few. Before you get to the point of enjoying those benefits, however, college-bound athletes must register to establish an account. The NAIA is a similar but smaller entity with its own set of rules, regulations and eligibility center.

Why and how does my Rockstar register with the NCAA Eligibility Center?

The purpose of this process is to verify that each athlete is eligible to play as an amateur athlete. If you don't register, you will <u>not</u> be eligible to play or to be recruited. Fair enough?

17

Once you access the site
https://web3.ncaa.org/ecwr3/?DB_OEM_ID=9600
the registration process is fairly simple. The biggest thing is paying the $70 fee to receive your Rockstar's NCAA number. Some information can be submitted immediately, while other things will take a bit more time because they must come directly from your school or the standardized testing agency.

A few examples of what they'll request are:

- ACT or SAT scores

- grades

- high school information

- your sports participation history

- if you've ever been paid to play (that could be the difference between being an amateur or professional athlete)

The process doesn't take long, but once you finish (assuming you meet the standards) an NCAA # will be issued to you. If there is anything left undone, an automatic email request will usually be sent to your account as a reminder. From that point forward, you will include this number on all your communication with college coaches. You can place it just under your name in the closing of all your email correspondence.

How do you get started?

A simple email to the counseling office's administrative assistant got this ball rolling at my daughter's high school. They are usually very familiar with this process. It's best to request that the standardized testing agency send your scores at the time of test registration, as one of your four free options. For the ACT, your request is made by entering code 9999, which is the same process used to send reports to colleges. If you need to access the report post ACT registration, it's not a problem, you'll just have to pay about $15 to have them send it.

My athletes registered with the NCAA during their sophomore year in high school, but many do so their junior year.

CHAPTER 4

UNDERSTANDING LEVELS OF PLAY:
Athletic Associations & Divisions

"You have to learn the rules of the game. And then you have to play better than anyone else."
Albert Einstein

To be successful with the recruitment process, there are some background details that you must know about the different levels of play. Collegiate track operates under three basic associations: NCAA (National Collegiate Athletic Association), NAIA (National Association for Intercollegiate Athletics) and NJCAA (National Junior College Athletic Association) aka JUCO. Basically, these associations include colleges that are of a similar size and athletic competition level. What's more, each association has different funding and resources for their athletic programs and the level of competition and services are, for the most, in direct relation to that. While some of the higher profile track and field programs may participate in televised meets, others will compete in environments that may not seem much different than what goes on at your local high school track. Regardless of where you are, coaches are looking for athletes with good grades, a high level of commitment, discipline, work ethic and coachability. Oh, did I forget to mention athleticism? These elements become key in determining the best program fit for your Rockstar.

To help clarify matters a bit, I've included a brief description of each association and its special components. Plus, I've listed a few of the overall top performing track teams within each division and a chart with the first and eighth place performances for a few events at the corresponding 2018 championship meet. Please do not get discouraged by the numbers on these charts. Remember, these are the best of the best performances in each division level.

NCAA

As mentioned earlier, the NCAA is the largest association, which is broken down into three divisions. The basic differences in these divisions are the size of the school and the resources (budget) dedicated to athletic programs. This also often determines the skill level of the athlete the school is able to attract.

Division I schools are typically the most recognized athletic programs where student-athletes regularly compete at the highest level. In most cases, when the average Joe thinks of collegiate sports, they are usually more familiar with Division I schools. These are typically the schools whose football games you watch on tv each Saturday and whose hoodies your kids wear.

Similarly, Division II schools are medium sized with intermediate level of competition. Like Division I, Division II schools also offer athletic scholarships.

On the other hand, Division III schools include some of the top academic schools in the country, but they do not offer athletic scholarships. However, there are also athletic opportunities for student-athletes at these colleges and universities. Funding and financial packages for Division III student-athletes primarily include academic scholarships and grants.

Some examples of Division I schools:
The Ohio State University, University of Georgia, Texas A&M, University of Southern California, Stanford, University of Kentucky)

2018 Division I Outdoor Championship Results (1st and 8th Places)		
Event	Men	Women
100m	10.13-10.41	11.01-11.50
400m	43.61-46.2	49.80-52.23
1500m	3:44.77-3:56.12	4:08.75-4:12.36
Long Jump	27'5.5"- 25'9.5"	21'10.75-21'0.75"
Shot Put	67'7.5"-66'2.5"	62'10.75-56'0"

Some examples of Division II schools:

TAMU Kingsville, Ashland, Lincoln (Mo.), St. Augustine's, Grand Valley State

2018 Division II Outdoor Championship Results (1st and 8th Places)		
Event	Men	Women
100m	10.18	11.44
400m	45.35	52.05
1500m	3:45.34	4:22.02
Long Jump	26'2.25"-24'5.75"	20'9"-19'6.25"
Shot Put	62'8.75-58'1.75"	54'2.5-49'11"

Did you know that many HBCU's (historically black colleges and universities) compete at the Division II level?

Some examples of Division III schools:
Mount Union, North Central Illinois, George Fox, UMASS Boston, Wash U.

2018 Division II Outdoor Championship Results (1st and 8th Places)		
Event	Men	Women

23

100m	10.74-10.94	11.87-12.34
400m	46.07-47.98	54.09-55.64
1500m	3:50-3:55.79	4:25.08-4:33.98
Long Jump	26'0"-23'7.25	19'10.25-18'8"
Shot Put	61'1.25-53'2.25	52'1.25-45'1"

www.ncaa.org

Did you know that University of Chicago, MIT and Claremont-Mudd-Scripps are Division III schools? Yes, like I mentioned, some of the nation's top academic schools are in Division III.

NAIA

The NAIA is separated into two divisions. This association is much smaller than the NCAA and the level of play is most comparable to NCAA Division II athletics. Outside of size, one of the other biggest differences between NAIA and NCAA are the rules for the recruitment process. The NAIA athletic recruitment process is much more lenient on coaches and how early and often they can communicate with athletes.

Some examples of NAIA schools:
Wiley, Indiana Tech, University of British Columbia, Hastings, Wayland Baptist

To compete at this level athletes are required to *register with the* NAIA Clearinghouse.

2018 Division II Outdoor Championship Results (1st and 8th Places)		
Event	Men	Women
100m	10.35-10.74	11.68-12.21
400m	46.07-48.70	52.66-56.74
1500m	3:48.4-3:50.42	4:14-4:35.38
Long Jump	24'7.75-23'6"	20'6.25-18'9.25"
Shot Put	62'5.75"-55'9.25"	51'2.75-44'4.25"

www.naia.org

NJCAA

The NJCAA consists of the junior or community colleges. This is by far the smallest association of the three. These are two-year programs that include both academic and athletic opportunities. One of greatest benefits is that the NJCAA allows athletes who fall short of the academic standards to get another chance. These athletes can attend NJCAA schools for two years, get their grades up to par and then transfer to an NCAA or NAIA program. Many of these student-athletes could have been recruited to Division I programs based on their athleticism, but the academic standards posed a challenge for them. If your Rockstar finds himself in this category, then an NJCAA may be his best option to continue competing in track and field.

Some examples of NJCAA schools: Barton County, South Plains, New Mexico JC, Central Arizona

2018 Division II Outdoor Championship Results (1st and 8th Places)		
Event	Men	Women
100m	10.07-10.47	11.25-11.73
400m	45.51-47.63	53.44-56.31
1500m	3:57.89-4:04.45	4:42.34-4:58.90
Long Jump	25'7.25-23'4.5"	20'6.25"-18'3.25
Shot Put	60'10.5-52'8"	54'1.25-43'11"

www.njcaa.org

I've included a chart with is a basic breakdown to further help you differentiate in the skill level required to compete at various divisions. While there are other factors and details, this should give you a fair understanding of what you are dealing with. Take a look at the table below to get an idea of the options that are available:

Association	Type of School	# Schools	Length of Academic Program	Scholarship Types	Number of Track & Field Scholarships	Standards*
NCAA Div. I	large public universities	1200 divided between all NCAA Divisions	4-year schools	offers athletic and academic scholarship	Women: 18 per team	High athletic and academic standards *See school website
NCAA Div. I - Ivy League	Mostly small to moderate private institutions	8 schools	4-year schools	no athletic and no academic scholarship	N/A	academic excellence & selectivity in admissions *See school website
NCAA Div. II	52% public and 48% are private institutions	300 schools	4-year schools Athletic seasons for are slightly shorter than division I	Nearly 50% of student-athletes earn some type of athletically funded financial aid	12.6 per team	Athletic standard isn't as high as Div. I, High academic standards
NAIA	usually small private college	250+	4-year schools	offers athletic and academic scholarships	12 per team	athletic and academic standards aren't as high as with the NCAA
NCAA Div. III	usually small private colleges	1200 divided between all NCAA Divisions	4-year schools	only academic or non-athletic scholarships	N/A	
NJCAA	Community College	525	2 year (seeking option to transfer)	Scholarships can be hard to find at this level because many programs aren't fully funded	(M)up to 20 (F)	few (or no) academic requirements for acceptance

You may have noticed that the Ivy Conference was listed separate from the other Division I schools. This is because there are some unique circumstances as it relates to athletic recruitment at these schools. To do it justice, they will require a book of their own. Because of my experience with the Ivy recruitment process, I will address this separately. (see Appendix 5)

CHAPTER 5

WHY I'D RATHER BE A BIG FISH IN A SMALL POND, THAN A SMALL FISH IN A GIGANTIC OCEAN

"Your true value depends entirely on
what you are compared with."
Bob Wells

Understanding your Rockstar's true value as a prospective college athlete can be a real eye-opener.

It is easy to get caught up in the hoopla and local chatter of their athletic prowess and superiority in your hometown. I mean, he consistently places first in competitions, and he's been on a first name basis with the sports reporter at the local paper since middle school. Your Rockstar is clearly in a class of his own and a force to be reckoned with. Maybe, and maybe not. While these accomplishments are commendable, these successes do not necessarily equate to college recruitment, at least not how you may be thinking. Let me open your mind to something new.

There's a big world out there! With over 1800 schools offering athletic programs, your Rockstar is bound to find one that is suitable for his or her skillset. The key is not getting hooked on a specific program before you know what they can and are willing to offer. Repeat after me, "My goal is to help my Rockstar use their track skills to pay for college." Again, but this time, say it like you mean it, "My goal is to help my Rockstar use their track skills to pay for college." Great!

Understanding that means that you realize that your athlete may or may not compete at the Division I level and that is ok.

There are benefits to competing in each of the different associations and division levels. You will just have to help determine which works best for them. As I am writing this, my son is smack dab in the middle of the recruitment process for track and field. Thus far, he has been in communication with everything from Division III to Division I level programs, including Ivies and ACC. From our experiences, the Division III coaches tend to be a bit more aggressive in working to convince athletes of what they bring to the table, which is probably because they are lesser known for their sports programs. Remember, these schools do not offer athletic scholarships, so they focus on students with high academics. I mention this because some of the emails really make you take notice. One school talked about how the team is taking an international track and field trip to Havana, Cuba with no extra cost to the athletes. Another mentioned the close-knit, supportive community and personal interactions with faculty and staff. A few schools attach videos of various student-athletes' post college successes, which have included teammates starting a running apparel company, attending medical school, and one landing a dream job at an architecture firm designing zoos and amusement parks. These sound wonderful and are just a sample of what recruitment emails entail. Hopefully, this sheds some light on why your Rockstar should be open to the many opportunities that are available, regardless of whether the school is in the Division I category, or not.

Ultimately, when it comes down to it, your Rockstar may find that he prefers to come into a program in a position to score points as a "Big Fish" over joining a program where he will have to work his way up the ladder as a "small fish." These are decisions that he should feel confident in making by the time he finishes this book.

Tip: Division III schools do not typically offer official visits, but they can if your athlete is academically and athletically valuable for their program. In this case, the school would extend a travel voucher to the student-athlete.

31

CHAPTER 6

WHEN DOES THE RECRUITMENT PROCESS BEGIN?

"If opportunity doesn't knock, build a door."
Milton Berle

Ideally, the recruitment process should begin in ninth grade (if not then, there's no time like the present).

To be perfectly honest, there was a time when I would have smirked at the idea of beginning the college recruitment process as a freshman, because I had not yet discovered what I now know.

I get it, most ninth graders are running on the JV squad. They may just be getting their feet wet in terms of track and field.

Truth is, this may seem a bit early and maybe even premature for many, especially boys who haven't yet hit their growth spurt. But you must in fact realize that there is more to the recruitment puzzle than just your event times or marks. This would include researching colleges of interest online. It's not too early to begin visiting campuses to see what your Rockstar likes and where they feel most comfortable. This is how they'll begin making their target list of schools.

You should make a point of getting your Rockstar in a position to meet and chat with current student-athletes. A good place to start would be talking with recent graduates of their high school who are currently competing in college. Their high school track coach would be a good resource to connect him with some of his former student-athletes.

There are athletes attending schools that come in all sizes from religious affiliations, historically black colleges and universities, Ivy League schools, public and private, to name a few, where each group of athletes could genuinely share a piece of their experiences that may spark something in your child. At this point your Rockstar is green. The focus here is to get their mind churning on what type of environment in which they would feel successful as a student-athlete.

Here's the problem that often occurs when students are clueless about school options: your kid gets hooked on the record of one of the nation's football collegiate powerhouses, buys their logo emblazoned hoodie from Walmart and the next thing you know that's all they want to talk about. I'm guilty - Go Buckeyes!

However, after you visit the campus they discover their favorite college sports team has a campus that's too big or they don't offer their major. And remember, student first then athlete. Even worse, your Rockstar doesn't have an athletic profile that would warrant communication from a school on

33

this competitive level. It's a fiasco waiting to happen. Sure, they may shout about what they want and like, but the fact is, in most cases your Rockstar's experiences are too limited to make such an important decision at this stage in the game, so it's up to you to keep the doors wide open. My point - visit everywhere you can!

Unofficial Visits

Personally, my athletes started by visiting local campuses. We rode bikes across campus, took walking tours and found different reasons to just hang out around campuses as a family. Sounds creepy, but it wasn't. In fact, many non-students spend time on campuses, so it was not unusual, and we didn't feel out of place, but it did give the kids the tools to fairly judge which type of environment they like most. You can even use this time to check out the quality of the athletic facilities and take a quick trot around the track.

Later, we started incorporating campus visits into our travels. Whether we were visiting family for a holiday or competing in an out of town track meet, we made a point of checking out a local university or two. It just became a priority and it's actually a fun addition to any trip. Plus, we added donut stops to an on-or-near campus shop to make it more memorable. Some tours were scheduled while others were informal walks with a campus map in hand. Regardless, each experience served its purpose.

Tip: In case you've never scheduled a campus tour, it's pretty simple. Just google the university name. Look for a link that says future students or campus visits. From there, you should be able to follow the prompts and schedule a visit as a prospective student. It's free of charge and highly recommended. There's usually a limit of 6 guests that you can register, which in most cases works, but if necessary you can schedule as a group tour. These tours typically last anywhere from 1-2 hours and may include an admissions overview in addition to a student-led walking tour. Word of advice - make sure you keep your comfy shoes handy for these occasions.

In case you're wondering, this is not the same as an "official visit," which I will discuss later. In fact, chances are, you won't even see or meet the track coach while you're there. Honestly, I don't recommend even looking for the coach at this stage. Not to mention, if you're considering NCAA D1, you should know that the current rules prohibit coaches and athletic departments from participating in a student's unofficial visit, until they reach their junior year. Translation - no talking to coaches about recruitment before September 1st of Junior year, even if you just happen to be hanging out on campus. FYI, this rule doesn't apply to D2, D3 or NAIA schools. Understand that your goal for this visit is to get a feel for the academic opportunities, campus energy, students and like I mentioned before, to take a look at the athletic facilities. Keep it simple.

Other Ways of Knowing What's Out There

If you've never stepped foot on a college campus, don't worry. Outside of the unofficial visits that I've already discussed, there are many other ways to figure out what your Rockstar may want out of their college experience.

- Conduct online research by simply googling a university's name
- Use Virtual tour options on school websites
- Talk to past graduates of your high school who are student-athletes
- Participate in college fairs and Open Houses

CHAPTER 7

HOW TO RATE YOUR ATHLETIC ABILITY

The only place success comes before work
is in the dictionary."
Vince Lombardi, NFL Coach

Milesplit is a website that is going to become your go-to resource for high school track and field. I'm going to teach you to use it strategically to eradicate any question about where running opportunities exist for your athlete and how you can prove it.

While I'm sure you're an honest person of high integrity and have many people who would vouch for such, in the recruitment world, everything is about proof. Just because you say it, doesn't mean that it's so.

As a result, your next job is to make sure you have proof of everything you claim about your Rockstar's athletic ability. If you say he broke the school record, you better have a link to the meet showing the date and time of the event.

Thankfully, for your sake, there is Milesplit.

If you haven't heard of it or used it, don't worry, I'll bring you up to speed.

As you probably already know, Milesplit is a top track and field resource that automatically manages the athletic profile of most high school and some middle school student-athletes across the nation. It is an online resource that is dedicated to, available and accessible by track athletes, track coaches (middle, high school and college levels), and track fans. In fact, if you have internet access, you can google it now to take a look. For the most part, it is free to peruse.

Let me go a bit deeper on why this tool is so special.

Milesplit allows its viewers to isolate athletes based on characteristics such as graduation year, event, state, even by region to identify the top athletes in the desired category. For example, you can use the ranking feature to easily see how your 9th grade, male, 800m runner ranks against others 9th graders in the state of Ohio, as well as across the nation. This information is updated regularly and is probably the single most inclusive site for high school track athletes.

Milesplit creates a profile, which includes an athlete's name, high school or club team, and graduation year. Using data from your Rockstar's profile, Milesplit associates each athlete's performances with their name and adds the results of FAT (fully automated timing) competitions to their account. Dated results include event names and wind factors.

38

The quickest and easiest way to discover your Rockstar's value as a recruited track athlete is by searching their national ranking on Milesplit. Simply click a few links to find out where he stands within your state, nationally, or your national ranking within his graduating class. Remember, when it comes to recruitment, student-athletes are primarily being judged against other athletes in the same graduation year. These are the athletes your Rockstar is competing against for athletic scholarships and recruitment. The reason your Rockstar's national ranking is so important is because college coaches are recruiting nationally and internationally, not just in your home state.

Milesplit ranks athletes from fastest to slowest times. There are prompts on the ranking page of Milesplit that allow you to easily access this information. Plus, you can check this at any given point throughout the year.

Because there are so many track events and athletes across the nation, there are two site levels. The first is Milesplit USA, which mostly covers the fastest and the best, and national track news. The other is a state-level site which is managed by a webmaster/network at the local level. The information here is centered around events and athletes within the associated state. If you are a Trackhead, then you will love Milesplit, but you'll primarily use your state level site. Chances are you will be more familiar with the athletes and the news and discussions will be more relevant to you. Not only does Milesplit provide timely stories and accomplishments in track and field competitions, but it announces athlete signings, lists track camps, posts upcoming meets, and so much more.

Okay. Now let's take a look at the actual screen.

At the top of the screen you will see six tabs: Results, Rankings, Calendar, Coverage, Discuss, Registration and More. Without going into details on each of these, I recommend that you take a finger stroll through them on your own. For our purposes, and to keep things short and sweet, we're going to pay attention to Rankings and the little search icon off to the far right of the screen.

First, the Ranking feature is what truly sets track and field recruitment apart from any other sport.

What am I saying, you ask?

Like I've already mentioned, track athletes can always know where they stand against their graduating class. In most other sports, it is not so easy to know exactly where you rank against athletes nationally, because even in football there are other variables and intangibles in ranking athletes.

This is good news!

I recommend that you play with this ranking feature a while.

Now if you will slide over to the search prompt, we can take a look at another important feature that I want to share.

Simply type your Rockstar's first and last name in the search bar and click "search". This will allow you to gain access to their personal profile. Be advised, if your Rockstar has a fairly common name, you may discover there are multiple athletes across the nation who pop up on the list. This is not really a problem, but you may have to scroll down the page a bit to identify your Rockstar by their team or school name. Also, if your child runs in middle school, with a summer team and with their high school program there's a chance they could have at least three different accounts. This is not really a big deal either, but if you choose, you can contact Milesplit to merge them.

From here you can see that Milesplit stores a personal profile for each track athlete. The athlete's profile can be recognized by their name, high school, graduation year and the location of their high school. Over to the left, you'll notice the list of their fastest and best career performances at the top of the page. If you continue to scroll down, you will see more detail on each event in which they participated for a particular race and not just the best performance. There are other tabs on this screen that allow you to view their career progression and season bests. If Milesplit media or photographers have labeled any video, articles or meet pictures with this athlete's profile, this can also be accessed here.

41

Don't worry, you don't have to submit anything to your webmaster to get your Rockstar's profile going. Most FAT (fully automated timing) races are automatically uploaded to this website each time your Rockstar competes, regardless of location or event. Like I mentioned before, this resource is available to anyone who seeks to access it. I also noted that you don't have to submit anything, but you can choose to update your Rockstar's profile pic if you want. However, you will need to register with an account to have full access.

Now as far as the data, it is pretty accurate. In rare instances, a high school team may have a teammate run under your Rockstar's meet bib, which would put their time on your Rockstar's profile. This usually happens when there are last minute meet changes due to athlete injury, no show or a cancellation. The coaches may insert a different athlete into an event under your Rockstar's name, which is commonly a JV runner who wouldn't have had the chance to compete otherwise. What this means to you is that you may have an outlier, which is a faster or slower time than usual. This is a simple correction, but just an example to let you know that it is up to you and your Rockstar to manage the accuracy of this profile.

I didn't mean to bore (or hopefully excite) you with all this Milesplit info, but it is an essential tool for this recruitment process and I wanted to ensure that you feel confident using it.

The link to your Rockstar's Milesplit profile will be included on all your future communication with coaches. It provides the proof and detail of your Rockstar's performances that coaches accept and require.

> **Tip:** In the recruitment world, the more points an athlete has the potential to score, the more value they hold as a prospect. For example, sprinters can score in 100m and 200m open events and possibly two more relays. Distance runners are more valuable when they also compete in cross country.

CHAPTER 8

HOW TO FIND LOOPHOLES AND OPPORTUNITIES IN THE RECRUITMENT GAME AND PUT YOURSELF IN A BETTER POSITION TO BE RECRUITED

It's not the will to win that matters –
everyone has that.
It's the will to prepare to win that matters.
Paul "Bear" Bryant

The Track & Field Results Reporting System, more commonly known as TFRRS is your secret weapon. You can think of it as the big brother to Milesplit. This site stores results and athletic performances for all collegiate track and field athletes and teams. It covers NCAA, NAIA and more.

TFRRS is where you will find your pot of gold in terms of easily and quickly sorting through actual and current team data and statistics at the conference, regional and national levels.

It has information compiled in the form of leaderboards for each event, team rosters as well as links to individual profiles for each athlete on any team across the nation. All this data is in one centralized location which can be filtered by conference, team and event.

What does that mean to you, you ask?

- ✓ Identify a need on a target team: You can quickly and easily review last season's athlete performances at your target schools to see how many athletes are competing in your event.

- ✓ Reveal Position Openings: You can also, instantly identify schools who may be in need of an athlete of your talents due to graduating seniors.

- ✓ Uncover hidden opportunities: If you rely on recruitment standards data alone, you could easily miss out on a potential opportunity.

In some cases, you may notice that regardless of size or conference, colleges and universities list certain scholarship standards in an event, but none of their athletes meet the standard. Simply put, what a coach desires on paper may not be the reality of what they are able to recruit.

Moreover, if your 800m time will rank in the top eight finishers of the conference championship, while it may not meet their "scholarship standard," it slates you as a conference point scorer, and therefore of value to their track program. Their TFRRS team profile and conference results may reveal a loophole that creates an opportunity for your Rockstar.

To make the most of this tool, you'll need to click around a bit and check out different data. Typically, the latest results page will be the home page. If you scroll down, you will notice the track meets are dated, with most recent first. Look for the championship meets, which can be listed by association and division levels or by conferences.

If you are familiar with a conference, you can type the name into the search menu. Let's say you select the NCAA Division II Outdoor Championships. If you scroll down the page, you will see a list of all schools that competed in this division level. From here, you can click on any school to access their "top performances" or "all performances." Now, it is up to you to uncover potential opportunities for your Rockstar.

Tip: If you find a school fit, submit your email cover letter and Athlete Profile to every school in the conference. Oftentimes, these schools are similar in academic rigor and the level of athletic competition. A hidden gem may be discovered.

CHAPTER 9

CRITERIA FOR NARROWING LIST OF COLLEGES TO DETERMINE THE BEST FIT

"Having only one option is not an option."
Picture Quotes

Now that your Rockstar has visited a few campuses, conducted research and talked with current student athletes, it is time to create a target list. This is simply a list of schools that have potential, which should include a varied range from dream schools, close to home universities and out of state schools, to both small and large. Your Rockstar will want to cast their net far and wide because meeting both academic and athletic needs will require flexibility. It's also important to remember that coaches aren't recruiting for every event every year, and as a result may not have an opening for a prospect with your background. So, here are a few things to consider:

- Does the school offer my major and are the academics on par with my ability? Student first, athlete second says it all. Find a place that meets academic needs first.

- Where would I be happiest? The happiness factor is very important. This would include social life, the other students, activities and opportunities that are available outside of academics and track. Spending the next four years in a place that brings a smile to your face can be a big difference maker.

- What level of competition would be best for my talent level?

- Location, location, location. A list of preferences would help in this area - rural, urban, college town, close to home, near the ocean, etc.

STEP 2. RESEARCH TARGET LIST OF SCHOOLS

- Create a list of 30-40 schools

- Take unofficial visits to campuses (start locally then branch out)

- Use TFRRS to review performances of athletes from previous season

- Use Google spreadsheets to record your list or database of targeted schools

CHAPTER 10

MOST IMPORTANT YEAR: JUNIOR YEAR

"To be prepared is half the victory"
Miguel De Cervantes

It's no secret that junior year is the most important in the athletic recruitment game. This is the year for your Rockstar to run their best times, jump their longest distances and heights, or throw their furthest.

By the third year of high school, your Rockstar is a seasoned athlete. Their bodies are stronger, maturity and athletic perspective has developed, and leadership opportunities are available on the team and in the academic realm of which they should take advantage. So, if your Rockstar was waiting for their senior year to "peak" please get that craziness out of your head. If all is timed well, by the time they complete their junior year of competition, which can include summer track meets, your Rockstar should be in a recruitable position.

By this point, both parent and athlete must be aware of the times, event marks, and academic admission criteria that are necessary for recruitment to their college choice. As a parent, you must know how important it is for your Rockstar to already have their ducks in a row. This can really put your athlete on easy street.

Benefits you can expect:

- By the time July 1st rolls around, you are ready to communicate with your dream school's coach

- Takes pressure off you during the chaos of senior year

- Allows you to enjoy your visits without the stress of "hitting that elusive time" hanging over your head

- You become eligible for Early Decision if you are confident about your school choice

Remember, eyebrows are raised based on your 9th and 10th grade performances, but calls are made from your 11th grade results. September 1st marks the official date that Division I college coaches can contact you, and you want to be ready.

Let me explain.

The summer following my daughter's Junior year in high school, we stopped coaching our summer track team. We had arranged her summer competition calendar in advance and knew that it would be impossible and unfair to coach a youth team and meet the demands of her out of state travel schedule. And if that's not enough, she had changed from running the 800m to 400m intermediate hurdles. With this

51

new event complicated by stringent time constraints, she needed intense training. She was, in fact, our priority, and time was dwindling, so we had to adjust. The result? Her track performances during that summer were key to her recruitment. No doubt about it, we made the right decision.

To show you what I mean, after running her PR (personal record) in the event, doors opened immediately. In fact, the first coach she spoke with in person was, at the time, her number one choice. It was right after she completed the finals of her event at the USATF Junior Olympics in Sacramento.

The coach was there checking out prospects, and she had just run within their qualifying hurdles standard for recruitment. We had previously researched the current athletes on that collegiate team who compete in the same event, so we were fully aware of her status and his possible interest. Although there was a small herd of athletes and parents vying for his time, he was patient and open to speaking with her. Their discussion included questions about her athletics and academic background, which would all be important factors in determining her eligibility with their program. His questions included gpa, community service, leadership, extracurricular involvement, academic rigor (AP/Honors courses), class rank, as well as ACT/SAT scores. He confirmed that based on the information provided, she met the qualifications of what they look for in a student-athlete. He then shared a bit of advice on the college admissions essay process before moving on to the next athlete.

The interaction left us both hopeful and confused.

On one hand, were excited to learn that her academic and athletic profiles were acceptable, but on the other, we had no indication that her application would be supported by the coach. In terms of athletic recruitment, gaining verbal coach support is key.

Tip: All athletes should seek to hold a leadership position on their team. This reflects well on them in the eyes of coaches and college admissions teams. Serving as team captain by the junior or senior year of high school should be a goal.

CHAPTER 11

MEETING THE STANDARD

Never let the fear of striking out get in your way.
Babe Ruth

As I mentioned earlier, my husband AJ is a former collegiate track runner. He attended a Division I school but didn't take an ordinary route to get there.

Coming from a small rural town, which competed at the 1A-public level, his exposure was limited. AJ used to tell us a story about his high school track days when he competed against an athlete who had the reputation of running with his heart in his pocket. I think that was a way of describing an athlete whose desire and talent far surpassed any other's they had encountered. Well, on the day of their regional meet, that athlete must have had a hole in his shorts (and his heart fell thru it), because all eyes were on AJ as he edged out the other athlete to win the race. Based on this performance and others, it was clear that AJ had a love for running and he certainly showed potential. He was, in fact, a local champion.

However, with little guidance, he had no thoughts nor had anyone else ever mentioned anything to him about the possibility of being a collegiate athlete. Plus, although he stood out as a top athlete in his area, his times weren't near scholarship level. In fact, he had earned and accepted an ROTC scholarship to pay for his college expenses.

Well, a few weeks after he arrived at his new university, AJ got the running itch again, and decided to join in on a practice session. Crazy enough, the coach liked what he saw and allowed AJ to continue training with the team. I guess he was "running with his heart in his pocket," because before long, AJ was recognized as one of the top middle-distance athletes on the team. By second semester, the coach offered him a scholarship. The rest is history.

I told you this story to give you a clearer perspective on a make or break factor that will determine if your Rockstar is truly in a position to be recruited and at what level. If I'm not mistaken I've already introduced the term qualifying standards for recruitment or recruiting standards, but they warrant further explanation.

You may be surprised to learn that each school has a predetermined list of times, distances and heights that high school athletes must achieve in order to be considered for their athletic team. In most cases you can easily google "(insert the school name) track and field scholarship standards" to access this document.

You'll see these standards are divided into three basic levels: Target Recruits, Scholarship Standard and Walk-On Standard.

Here's how it works,

Target Recruit

"Target Recruit" level requires the highest standard of achievement because based on this athlete's profile, they can typically make an immediate impact in terms of scoring points for their team at the conference or national levels.

News flash!

What coaches are really looking for are athletes who come in primed to score points at the conference level.

As you might imagine, these student-athletes typically rank in the top 10 nationally of the prospective event within their graduating athletic class, and in some cases are already household names for Trackheads. And don't overlook the fact that some of these athletes may have also represented their country on the international level as a high school student.

Scholarship Standard

The next level is the Scholarship Standard. This level identifies student athletes who will probably receive a percentage of support from the university based on their athletic performances.

These athletes may score conference points but are less likely to score national points during their freshman year. They

56

have probably won high school state championships or at least placed within the top three medal winners. Chances are high that these track athletes compete and train with club teams and have earned medals in national level competitions such as USATF/AAU Junior Olympics.

This group is represented by a much larger percentage of athletes than Target Recruits, but still represents top tier athletes.

Walk-On

The third group represents an even larger group of potential candidates and is composed of those who have met the "Walk-On Standard."

These athletes come from a host of different backgrounds. They could range from state podium making athletes who place in the 4-8th positions, school athletes who have not competed at club level or worked with specialty coaches, or athletes from single A – AAA* track programs who consistently win but have limited competition throughout their season, to name a few.

Based on their high school performances these students are allowed to train and compete with the team, but they do not receive scholarship money. With proven results, there are instances where Walk-On athletes are able to transition to earning a scholarship, like AJ, but it may not be very common.

As you can see, coming from such a small environment with only a few races under his belt, AJ was in a unique situation. His best high school times didn't meet the Walk-On Standard. However, once he was in position to train at a higher level, his desire, hard work and talent allowed him to jump up to scholarship level.

In terms of your Rockstar, this is where the rubber meets the road. Knowing what you now know about recruiting standards, you can strategically use Milesplit and other factors to see where your athlete fits best. Once you know that it's time to reach out to coaches.

Tip: Accepting the role of a Walk-On athlete should not be taken lightly. Faced with all the challenges and demands of life as a student-athlete, with few or none of the benefits and possibly no chance of earning aid for running is serious business. Remember, most campuses also have less demanding options which include intramural and club sports for the students who love to run and compete.

This is not to suggest that top talent does not come from smaller athletic regions, because there are many who excel regardless of the level in which they compete.

CHAPTER 12

STEP 3: CREATE ATHLETIC PROFILE

"Why fit in when you were born to Stand Out"
Dr. Seuss

It's no secret that coaches have an inbox full of messages from athletes. It's their job to sift through these emails to find the best prospects for their team.

At the same time, it's your Rockstar's job to stand out and be remembered.

That's why the Athletic Profile is so important. No, I'm not talking about your profile on Milesplit or a link that you've set up with a recruiting company. This is a one-page resume that I'm going to teach you to create. It highlights the best of what your Rockstar has to offer and will be attached to the initial contact email that is sent to each target school.

It will contain such information as athletic and academic accomplishments, your Rockstar's personal and school contact information, as well as a brief summary of their strengths and potential. Don't worry, this can be created on your home computer and no flashy decorations are needed.

The Athletic Profile should be:

- Neatly organized and easy to read
- Truthful in describing your Rockstar's accomplishments
- Able to fit into one page
- Save as a pdf

It should include the following information:

Section 1: Name, graduation year, and track & field event (big and bold) - with a headshot of you (not in your uniform)

Section 2: Catchy header that features your Rockstar's most important athletic highlight/accomplishment

Section 3: Contact information - address, phone, email, dob, height* & weight* (*only include if you believe it works in your athlete's favor)

Section 4: Academic information - school name, address, phone, gpa, class rank and size, standardized test name and score

Section 5: Academic highlights - awards, honors, internships, leadership

Section 6: About Me: Write a concise paragraph that shares something personal about who you are, what drives you to compete, and describe your strengths and future athletic potential. This is where you can mention any family members, especially those who are or were collegiate athletes. You may also want to identify any other sports that you have participated in as a high school student, particularly if you played on the varsity level. Your intended college major should also be identified.

Section 7: Athletic Highlights - track and field awards, honors, school/state/national records, leadership, identify national meets in which you have participated

Section 8: PRs - list your personal best times for your events and the year that you earned the time. Also include your NCAA # in this section.

Optional information to ensure a full page: coach contact info (high school or summer), school counselor contact info, positive quotes from your coach about your abilities/practice habits/attitude, community service

If you need more to understand this step, please check out the companion workbook which shows a detailed sample template.

Tip: You can use the "insert table" feature in Google Docs so that each section is separated and neatly organized. This also allows you to easily highlight certain sections to capture the coach's attention. Most of the information will be in list form, except for the "About Me" section.

A successful Athletic Profile will build an initial connection between you and the coach, and hopefully open the door to further communication.

Jon Smith

Insert Your
Rockstar's
Photo

℅ 2020 Track & Field (800m)

Contact Info:
555 Champions Drive
My Town, OH 44122
(216) 555-5555
jonsmith2010@gmail.com

Lucky High School
My Town, OH 44122
Enrollment 1411
Graduation: May 2020
GPA: 3.63
Rank: 17/362
ACT: 26 Composite

ACADEMIC HIGHLIGHTS:

Math Dual Enrollment
SGA Treasurer
National Honor Society
Spanish Club

Other:
XYZ Church Youth Group
Volunteer Club of America
100 hours of community service

About Me: I have been running since the age of 8, and I plan to continue at the collegiate level because I find the sport fun yet challenging. My combination of speed and endurance are key. This year, I plan to lead my team to the podium at the state championship. As a collegiate athlete, I will bring discipline, a strong work ethic and a desire to be my best while helping my team to do the same. I plan to major in Math.

Cara D. Jackson

ATHLETIC HIGHLIGHTS

Track & Field	Personal Best
2016, 2017, 2018 All State	Times
2018 All Region	
2017 4x400 6th Place - State	200m 22.85
Championship	400m 48.6
2018 4x400 5th Place - State	800m 1:54
Championship	5K 16:21
2017, 2018 Team Captain	

HS Record Holder	**NCAA#:**
4x400R - 3:18 (2016)	**5555555555**
4x800R - 8:11.37 (2016)	

*Video is available upon request

CHAPTER 13

WHEN & HOW TO COMMUNICATE WITH COACHES

*"You can't cross the sea by merely standing
and staring at the water."*
Rabindranath Tagore

The results are in, it's time to contact coaches!

As your Rockstar progresses it will become increasingly important to track and promote their accomplishments. The Promote 'em Like a Rockstar process will show three different ways to do so. The first is optional for track athletes, while the other two are essential to making this system work:

1. Social Media

2. Email

3. Phone

I'm sure you can attest that very few people achieve success without a plan, and the track recruitment process is no different. No, I'm not suggesting that you draw up a glossy 8.5x11" manual. However, you will need to follow a simple strategy of attack to manage your communication with coaches that will keep you on the right course to make your Rockstar's dream a reality.

Here's what you'll need:

- To use your dedicated Gmail account for sending all messages
- To create a database of coaches' contact information and correspondence using Google Sheets

- The notebook that was mentioned earlier to record all verbal communication

Using Social Media in the Recruitment Process
Let's say as a freshman, your Rockstar has a breakout season. He starts on varsity and is a team leader in terms of performance. If this is the case, you can go a bit deeper. Believe it or not, it's social media time.

Post, retweet, favorite, like and share!

A simple picture of your Rockstar on the podium speaks volumes. Tweeting that they set a school record or won a major meet is also a great way to build momentum. For example, "Freshman 800m runner breaks school record in 1:56." Posting a note about an academic achievement or award is equally significant.

These snippets are great ways to begin promoting your Rockstar. It's simply using a compelling headline. What I mean by that is using social media is a great opportunity to feature some of their highlights.

There's no question of the benefits of these platforms in networking with followers, liking and sharing other users' posts, even creating recruitment battles (that's more likely a football thing). Bottomline, they connect us to the world.

On some levels, finger tapping on a screen is more common than talking. With that in mind, setting up Twitter, Facebook, YouTube and/or an Instagram account is a good start, but before they leap, you must be smart and guide your Rockstar.

This must be done strategically. Haven't you seen stories about athletes and public figures misuse or getting caught posting inappropriate or offensive comments on social media? It's not uncommon, because these accounts are open to public view.

Really, in order to benefit in terms of recruitment purposes from the account, it must be set up as a public account, not private. In fact, it may be wise to create a separate personal account, so that your recruitment account is strictly business.

All I'm saying is that it's imperative that your Rockstar understands that these posts are open game to anyone who accesses their account, including coaches. That means no profanity, racist or sexist comments, tagging vulgar images or overall questionable content that you wouldn't say if the coach was sitting next to you on your living room sofa. Believe it or not, coaches are scanning accounts just like anyone else.

Remember, this is where your managing responsibility is crucial. You don't have to send the communication. Your Rockstar can and should post, but you must oversee the process to ensure it is clean and consistent with the image and reputation that you are building.

Enough about what your Rockstar shouldn't do, let's talk about what they should.

67

- Create a username that would make your grandmother proud
- Build a profile that will promote your Rockstar attributes in a way that makes a great first impression
- Actively tweet, post, like and share your accomplishments, articles and videos
- Upload YouTube videos of your meet performances, training regimen, and clips showing your skills
- Associate with your coaches/teams of interest -Follow on Twitter, Fan on Facebook
- Use links to connect and promote one account with another (i.e., YouTube link on Facebook page)

Just so you know, coaches won't comment or respond to your posts or interact with you through your accounts, but they do see them. This is because there are NCAA rules that prohibit them from doing so until you've committed to attend their school. Nonetheless, this might be their first impression of you even before the first email.

The most important thing to remember is that your job is to create buzz that will attract college coaches that recruit and offer money for school. It's as simple as that!

CHAPTER 14

STEP 4: Emailing Coaches: What, When & How

"There is no perfect formula for email - authentic and honest messaging works"
Quoteprism

As your Rockstar progresses it will become increasingly important to track and promote their accomplishments.

This is where knowing what, when and how to contact coaches by email becomes critically important.

My daughter ended her sophomore year on the state championship podium and as the predicted 800-meter state champion for the upcoming year. Pending no phenoms joined her region, it was pretty much a done deal that she would win. Knowing this, she was able to capitalize on this highlight. So, in the header of an email, which included a summary of her profile and a link to Milesplit, a message was sent to several coaches of schools in which she had expressed an interest. The email looked like this:

Subject: Entering 2016 season as #1 ranked 800m runner for 4AAAA

Message: Please check out my daughter's track profile. University X is her #1 dream school (or "she could be an asset to your track and field program").

Susan Smith
Lucky High School
c/o 2017 (currently a junior)
800m: 2:16
Rank: 17/323
GPA: 3.4 (on 4.0 scale)
ACT: 26 (will retake)

2X All-state, 3x Region Champion and 3x County Champion and All Conference selection.

Please continue to keep an eye out on her stats
(insert Milesplit link)

This season she is working to reach a 2:10 or better.

Thank you!

Father Smith

While this first email came from a parent, any further communication should come from the student.

Understanding what, when and how you email is crucial to the recruitment process.

In most cases, email is the first direct contact your Rockstar will have with a coach. One mistake you don't want to make is to botch it up.

Anytime your Rockstar has a highlight, share it! They don't have to write a dissertation, just drop a quick email to their list of coaches that briefly describes how they have been awesome.

Remember, it's a trailer not the movie. Also, when I say anytime, I don't mean multiple emails in a week's time. I'm talking every few weeks or months, in season. It's just a tidbit to let them simmer on the potential of what your Rockstar may bring to their program. If you're hungry to send more, shout it out on social media instead.

This step is valuable for a few reasons. One, just like a movie trailer, it plants a seed in their mind to look out for your Rockstar. Two, if they are interested, it could open the door for back and forth conversation down the line. Three, if done properly, you can begin gaining a clearer idea about the programs where your Rockstar may actually have a future.

In the early stage, these emails are similar to tweeting a highlight. It's too early for them to provide feedback, but it could put you on the coach's radar.

71

By the end of Junior year, your email approach will evolve a bit. Now, you are in a position to spark conversation with a coach. The new objective is not just to get a look, but to get a response. Your emails have to be targeted to accomplish this goal.

5 elements to maximum effectiveness and success in getting coaches to open and respond to your email

- **Element#1 Be specific by using the coach's name.** Do your research beforehand, because no coach wants to receive a message that looks like it was sent in bulk mail. You should go on the school's track website, which can be easily googled ("school name" track and field). Access the list of coaches. There are typically multiple coaches on any track team's staff, with the head coach listed first. You want to read the bio of each coach so that you can become familiar with the staff and gain insight on their background and possibly coaching priorities. Next, you will identify your event specific coach. This is the person you email! They will be most familiar with your event and will ultimately be the one who dedicates the most time to recruiting you when the time comes. Sidebar - some smaller schools do not have a recruiting staff, and in such cases, you will direct your email to the Assistant Coach.

- **Element #2 Know the team.** Too often students email coaches having no idea of the team needs. If they just recruited four athletes' in your event, there's a fair chance there won't be an opening for you in the upcoming recruitment class. That's not to say that you shouldn't move forward with your email, but it's always good to be aware of potential roadblocks. While you're on the site, click on the team roster and access the appropriate gender list. You want to check out the current athletes who are competing in your event. Make a mental note of their personal records, best high school time and their graduation year. Are your current stats in range of their top high school performances? You should also count how many athletes on the team are in your event. If you notice that an athlete in your event is graduating soon, you could mention something about filling that need.

- **Element #3 Convey a lot using a little in your subject line.** This is key to getting your email opened and earning a response. You don't have to be flashy or wordy, but you should know that an estimated 47% of recipients decide to open an email based on subject line alone. Be brief, specific and include numbers (primary) or accomplishments (secondary). Since you're already familiar with the team needs, your subject line should cater to them. Check out these clickable samples: "2020 Male Sprinter, 10.7 200m" "2020 Female All-American Thrower" "1600m Female

73

State Champion 4:52, 2021." Notice that these subject lines are short, sweet and specific.

- **Element #4 Craft a professional Cover Letter that highlights your Rockstar's qualities.** In business it is estimated that employers spend 6 seconds on a resume before deciding to trash or interview. Coaches receive a lot of emails, so you want to make your 6 seconds count. Get in, deliver the package, and get out. Your content should look similar to this:

Dear Coach Smith,

What does it take to be a Buckeye! I am a high school junior in Bedford, Ohio, and a state champion 200m runner. I am interested in the chemical engineering program at OSU and being a part of the track team. I've included my stats below.

100m:
200m:
LJ:
GPA:
Rank: (out of __)
ACT Composite Score:

I have also attached my athletic profile, to give you a better idea of who I am and how I can

74

contribute to Ohio State's track and field program.

FYI- I will be competing at the Taco Bell Meet next week

Respectfully,

Your Name
Graduation Year
Link to Milesplit account
Phone number (make sure this is a number that will be answered)

This is simple and to the point. It touches on your academic and athletic achievements and goals and leaves the door open for further communication to come. Make sure the times and marks listed are your personal records. If your profile is in range with this coach's needs, chances are high that he will reply.

Notice what we did not do and why:

#1 <u>We did not</u> Write a five-paragraph essay - be respectful of the coach's time

#2 <u>We did not</u> Open with "Dear Coach" - too impersonal

75

#3 We did not List all our extracurriculars - too much too soon

#4 We did not Attach our transcript or ACT score report - give them something to ask you for in their reply. It gets the ball rolling.

#5 We did not Add video - see #4, if they're interested they'll ask

- **Element #5 Review, review, review.** Did I say review? I recommend typing the content first and applying the coach's email address last (after reviewing it) to prevents an accidental send. This is the point where mom or dad comes in to double check misspellings, content and general appropriateness of the message. If you read it aloud it's easier to detect errors.

Tip: An easy way to express your interest further is to mention that you have visited the campus, watched the team compete in person, participated in an on-campus academic program or you can acknowledge a success that the team has achieved.

Now that you have this step down, your Rockstar is going to repeat it for each college of interest. Please do not get caught cutting and inserting coach's names on a generic template. It will not work out in your favor if an error goes undetected during your review. If it seems like a lot to follow these steps for each school, maybe your Rockstar needs to reconsider just how serious they are about that team.

Let's talk about why these emails need to come from your Rockstar and not you. This is an important step in managing your Rockstar and managing yourself. Beware! Many coaches do not look favorably upon parents emailing them. Let's face it, it may seem easier, but in the end, it doesn't benefit your Rockstar. Not only is it their responsibility, but it is your opportunity to train your Rockstar to communicate professionally and advocate on their own behalf. Remember, if all goes well they will not only have to send emails but hold a conversation with their potential coach, on the phone and in person. If I'm not mistaken, that is the end goal.

Thinking back to when my daughter was going through this process, a friend sent us a sample email that he had used to initiate conversation about his daughter. He simply got the ball rolling and then put his daughter in the driver's seat. We followed his template and it worked!

The only thing left, is to attach your Athletic Profile to your email and send! Remember, putting your face and story in front of the coach personalizes the message.

CHAPTER 15

WHAT HAPPENS AFTER A COACH RECEIVES YOUR EMAIL?

After a coach receives your email, it is a good sign when you get an emailed response. It lets you know that your message has been opened and it peaked their interest. Yay!

The coach's response may include a request for you to do one or more of the following:

Possible Request #1: Complete a Prospect Questionnaire
This is an online tool that every college and university has for their track program. It is used to get the nitty-gritty on your Rockstar. While some choose to complete these ahead of time, I recommend waiting until the coach requests it. Questionnaires tend to be long and time-consuming to fill out because typically, single prompt answers are required (translation - no 'cut and paste'). Typing 50 questionnaires without coach interest isn't my idea of a fun evening, but the choice is yours.

So, when a coach requests it, your Rockstar should get to work immediately. However, it would be helpful to have a few items handy:

✓ High school transcript

✓ Event PR (personal records) with race dates and location

✓ High school contact information including that of your coach and counselor

✓ Standardized test score report

✓ NCAA #

Possible Request #2: Submit a video of your Rockstar in action

A video can deliver aspects of your athleticism and intrinsic qualities that numbers alone cannot express. Maybe your technical skills need work, but you show determination and drive. How do you hold up at the end of your race? Your stats may be borderline, but a video can allow a coach to recognize your potential. The Rockstar Promoter should be recording videos each time the athlete competes. Again, unlike football, this doesn't have to be fancy. It can be recorded on your cell phone or you can upload your videos to YouTube.

Tips about the video:

- No need to add music or special effects

- Refrain from loud talking or cheering in the background

- Clear and steady images are necessary (in racing events, be sure to identify your Rockstar)

- Your Rockstar should be a top finisher in the event if not the winner

- Track events are short. Begin recording from setup to finish (this way the coach can observe mechanics and protocol followed prior to actually running, jumping or throwing)

- If possible, include a shot of the timing screen showing your Rockstar's name and results

Possible Request #3: Schedule a phone conversation
Most coaches won't bother talking with you over the phone if they're not pretty serious. This doesn't mean that the deal is sealed, but it is a great feeling to reach this point. This is a big step, so I've dedicated an entire chapter to the phone call.

Nonetheless, any one of the aforementioned responses is high-five worthy!

<u>Tip:</u> Opportunities may come out of nowhere. My son emailed his info to a high academic Division I school who indicated that they did not have an opening for his skill. A few days later, two Division III coaches of similar academic standards emailed him expressing interest. They said his information was forwarded by the Division I coach.

"People may hear your words, but they feel your attitude"
- John C. Maxwell

The Phone Call: What to Say, What Not to Say and When
So, when my daughter received a coach's email requesting the best time to talk, our entire household was ecstatic. This was our first experience, but for whatever reason, we felt like the phone call represented the turning point at which she would soon move from being a prospect to an actual recruit.

Like most calls, it was scheduled in the evening around 7 p.m., so as to not interfere with high school classes or practice time. In anticipation of the call, we began scouring the internet for questions to ask and information on what to expect. Just before the scheduled call, my daughter grabbed a pen and notebook to jot down the questions, and to have paper available to record details from the conversation. I recommend that you get a dedicated notebook to record details from your calls. Your Rockstar should date and jot down notes throughout the conversation. If both hands are needed, most coaches are fine with being on speaker phone.

Tip: If the phone is on speaker parents can listen but should not intervene in the conversation unless the coach specifically requests information from you.

Hold on a moment before making that call. There are a few important factors that will help your Rockstar impress the coach and relieve anxiety.

81

- First, they should review the coach's bio on the team website to refresh their memory and gather a few talking points.

- It would also be helpful to check out the team performance from the previous year, particularly in the conference championship meet. This could also be a conversation starter.

- One thing you should also remember is to express your gratitude for being considered as a prospect to compete for (insert school name).

- Rehearsing the call with a parent or other adult can be helpful.

- Last, having a handy list of 10-12 questions is another way to be organized and confident.

CHAPTER 16

STEP 5. THE PHONE CALL: What to Say and What Not to Say

"An idea not coupled with action will never get any bigger than the brain cell it occupied."
-Arnold Glasow

Okay, so let's talk about what to do if a coach wants to talk with your Rockstar over the phone. This is a big deal. Once you get to this point, you both deserve a pat on the back, because this is when the process gets "real".

However, you will most certainly need to prepare before chatting it up on the phone with your potential future coach. You should start by writing down a few questions to ask.

Here are a few things to consider:

1. I recommend starting by **getting to know the coach on a more personal level**. Your Rockstar can simply ask about his family, hobbies outside of track, pets, personal experience as a track athlete, etc. These conversations can easily be all about the athlete, this is also time for your Rockstar to find out if this is a person with whom he/she can work well. They'll definitely

want to ask about his coaching philosophy for your event(s) and team goals for the upcoming season.

2. Next, the conversation should naturally transition into **general questions about the program and team dynamics.** Find out about practice times and duration, off-season training expectations, and academic resources available to student-athletes (especially tutors). Ask if athletes live together in the dorms or how the school typically handles living arrangements for student-athletes. Your Rockstar could ask about whether the team does any bonding activities or takes special trips together. It's also important to ask about the facilities and athletic resources (i.e. tutoring).

3. The last line of questioning will **be more focused on your Rockstar's future there as a student-athlete.** They'll want to find out about how the coach plans to use their talents to benefit the team. What will be their role? It's equally important to know where your Rockstar stand on his recruitment list, because he is undoubtedly recruiting other athletes for the same event. Will your Rockstar compete as a freshman?

4. The coach may ask about other schools your Rockstar is considering. They should **be honest** but wise in answering this question. Their response could reveal a lot, especially if they have no other potentials. Assuming that is not the case, the best answers are to name other schools within that coach's athletic

84

conference. Lesser programs usually don't create negotiating opportunities, but in conference teams can create leverage.

5. To close out your conversation, you'll first ask if the coach has any additional questions. If not, you'll thank him for his time and ask the most important question, **"what is the next step in this process?"**

Typically, the coach will lead the conversation and the student will follow accordingly.

Tip: It may seem old-fashioned, but students should use "yes" or "yes sir" (or "yes ma'am") instead of yeah when communicating with coaches. Showing respect can go a long way in gaining favor from an adult.

After the call, what should you expect?

If all goes well, the coach may be interested in having you come in for an "official visit".

Realistically, there are usually a few phone conversations before the official visit offer is extended.

Before a visit can happen, the coach will request a few items from you so that the admissions office can perform what is called a Pre-read. You should always respond promptly to a coach's requests.

Here is what you will need to provide (in pdf format) for a Pre-read, in most cases:

- Transcripts through your junior year
- A list of your senior year classes specifying AP, Honors, etc.
- A copy of your official ACT or SAT score report
- Some institutions will ask for a school profile (this can be requested from your high school's counseling office)

The coach will submit these items to the admissions department to verify that you meet the minimum standards as set by the college or university. It may take a day or in some cases a few weeks to hear back.

The admissions department will be checking to ensure:

- that you have completed the required core courses
- your grades meet or exceed the minimum requirement
- your test scores are within the minimum range or better
- your senior year classes are of required rigor and fulfill any unmet needs in the core requirements

This is the first barrier that you must cross.

Then, once the school's admissions department approves your documents, they'll want to do an early financial needs analysis. Forms such as the CSS Profile, W-2s and tax returns will be requested. All this information will be used to determine the cost of your academic experience and the estimated family contribution (the amount you will have to pay). After review, this information will be compiled in the form of a financial award letter.

Remember, the key college expenses include:

- Tuition and fees
- Room and board
- Books and supplies
- Personal expenses
- Transportation

If all goes well with the school's review of your documents, the next step is to schedule the official visit.

Tip: Coaches are usually in communication with at least four athletes for one event. The second or third call would be a good time for your Rockstar to find out where they rank on the coach's depth chart of prospective athletes.

CHAPTER 17

STEP 6: OFFICIAL VISITS

*"What the mind of man can conceive
and believe, it can achieve."*
Napoleon Hill

Like any Rockstar deserves and for fun's sake, let's think of the campus visit like a promotional tour or talk show interview. This is when your Rockstar gets the chance to really find out about the school and to show the coaching staff that they are worth the hype. But let's first take a closer look at Official versus Unofficial visits. There is a big difference.

In short, the primary difference is who foots the bill. The NCAA sets the rules and regulations for both types of visits. In a nutshell, unofficial visits are unlimited, not paid for by the school, and are arranged by someone other than a school representative, such as the athlete's family. It's a chance for you to check the lay of the land on your own, to find out if it's a place you could see yourself in the future.

A recent addition to NCAA rules for Division I programs prohibits coaches from participating in an athlete's unofficial visit before September 1st of their junior year. Other than that, unofficial visits are pretty much the same as any nonathlete would experience. For the most part, the strict rules apply to official visits, so that is where we will focus our time.

What happens on an official visit

In my daughter's case, this was the first time she had met any member of the recruiting team's coaching staff in person. So not only was this an opportunity for them to check her out, but it was equally important for her to do the same. Don't be fooled, the recruiting university has a protocol. This is new to you, but not them. They really make a point of putting their best foot forward to make your Rockstar have a memorable and positive experience. Obviously! Their goal is to get you to say "yes!" But don't be fooled into thinking that you aren't under the microscope, because the coach and your student-athlete host are assessing your character, how you fit in with the team and your attitude.

To give you a good idea of how this works, I'll share my daughter's first "official visit" experience.

After about the third call, the event coach insisted that she speak with the head coach. This was a sign that he was serious about her as a recruit and the process was progressing as planned. The call was shorter and had a more serious tone than her usual conversations with the event coach. Soon after the call, she was contacted about scheduling an official visit. The coach offered a few dates, and after checking her calendar, my daughter agreed to one. It's important to note that we had already received an Early Estimated Financial Aid

Eligibility document from the school's office of financial aid. I'm telling you this, because the school wanted to make sure that my daughter not only had met the academic standards for admission, but that we clearly understood our financial responsibility before they brought her on campus. This is common with Ivy recruitment.

The NCAA allows <u>five</u> official visits (one visit per school) and this was going to be her first. Some advise using all five visits, while others suggest that 3-4 is enough. While it may seem fun at first, the visit process can be draining and sometimes interfere with senior year coursework. My recommendation is to use your best judgement but try to visit as many schools as possible. The first visit is always exciting because it's a new experience. However, you must remember your goal is to see where you truly fit in best, so you need to have something to compare.

A few days passed and then a plane ticket was emailed. She was scheduled to arrive on a Saturday as agreed and depart on Monday. Here's why: the NCAA has strict guidelines governing official visits. Schools have up to 48 hours to convince recruits that their school is the best choice. Visits generally include campus tours, overnight stays in a dorm room with a student athlete, sitting in on class sessions, and at some schools up to 3 free tickets to a school sporting event.

My husband and I bought our own airline tickets and fortunately we were able to join my daughter on her flight.

Our instruction was to look for a white van when we landed. Upon exiting baggage claim, we spotted it and the coach. We were the last to board the van, which was already occupied by a few other prospective athletes, most who were not accompanied by their parents. Everyone was fairly quiet during the drive to campus which gave us an opportunity to check out the surrounding city. As we approached the university, the van dropped us off at a door which led directly into the athletic facility. We were escorted to the coaches' office area where after a brief "hiya doin" each student was partnered with a student-athlete host. This was the point at which parents went one way and students went another.

After dropping our items off at the hotel, my husband and I took the liberty to check out the surrounding area. As luck would have it, we ran into two familiar faces from the coaches' office. We discovered they were parents of another athlete who was on his second official visit. We were all very anxious to pick each other's brains about this experience and the recruiting process as a whole. They happened to be very excited about their previous visit and were already pointing out the good and the bad, while we had nothing to compare. We were fortunate to have found them and shared a table at a coffee shop until the wee hours of the morning chatting about how amazed we were about the opportunities available to our Rockstars. During that time, our kids did not contact any of us. We took that as a good sign.

91

The following day, we joined a formal campus tour, before meeting up with the athletes for a tour of the indoor track with a subsequent dinner. This was our first time actually joining with the other prospects. It happened to be a very large group of more than 20 athletes. Sidebar - on her second visit it was just my daughter and another student. Dinner was buffet style and khaki casual with all parents, prospects and coaching staff in attendance. At some point, the coaches personally introduced themselves to each family and individually fielded questions about our feelings thus far. As you might imagine, we were just happy to be there, especially since our daughter seemed to be enjoying her time and mingling well.

On Monday morning, once again we met as a large group for an informal session where we were introduced to the support team for the school's athletic program. They served a continental breakfast as the athletes sat around a large conference table. This was their chance to ask more questions, discuss any concerns and learn about the behind the scenes staff who are there to assist in making their experience a success. During this period, each athlete with parents in tow, was excused to privately meet with the head coach. This is when things turned serious. Without dilly-dallying, he got straight to the point and asked what we thought and what were my daughter's plans. Remember, they requested all of your information up front, so they already know that your Rockstar can be admitted to the program and it's now just a matter of deciding. At that time, my daughter had another scheduled visit and was still in communication with yet another of her top choices, so we were honest in letting him know. He asked for the date of the visit and scheduled a phone call just a few days after that to revisit this conversation. That call would be when she would have to make a verbal commitment, which would be to either accept or decline their offer. On one hand, seeing as this was one of her top choices, she was tempted to accept on the spot. Using her best judgement, she decided to wait. After speaking with the head coach, we had just a bit of time to observe an early season training session and say our farewells.

By 2pm, we were headed back to the airport for our return flight. On our way home, my daughter enthusiastically shared details about her experience hanging out with a few of the athletes off campus on Saturday night, as well as sleeping in the dorm. Both seemed to be positive. She now figuratively had a bird in the hand. And that's what this is all about!

Tip: When packing a bag for the visit, prospects should dress casually and wear comfortable shoes for walking. In some cases, school representatives will conduct interviews on the spot, so you probably don't want to make your first impression in a tank top and holey jeans. A bath towel and sleeping bag may also come in handy.

Questions Most Prospects Fail to Ask of Current Athletes:

1. If you could do it all over again, would you choose University X?

2. How do you balance your studying and free time with team commitments?

3. What can you tell me about your social life (friends, weekends, fun activities) outside of the track team? What did you do last weekend?

4. How do you feel about the team culture and the coach?

5. What are the most challenging aspects about being a student athlete at University X?

Tip: In some cases, first year students serve as hosts to prospective athletes. Since many official visits occur at the beginning of the school year, these students have clearly only been in school for a few weeks. Therefore, I recommend connecting with second year students and higher to ask any questions or address concerns.

Remember, if your Rockstar has options, they will need to consider all aspects of the program, including future teammates and the coach.

Chapter 18

ASSESSING TEAM FIT

"Sometimes the most ordinary things could be made extraordinary simply by doing them with the right people."
Nicholas Sparks

On my daughter's second official visit my husband escorted her, but I stayed home. A few hours after their arrival, I received a phone call from AJ. "You need to get up here to see this place." As he described his experience, I could see that this visit was much different than the previous one. First, the event coach picked them up from the airport, and this time it was just the three of them on board. AJ was set up in a nice campus hotel with a full parent agenda and enjoyed more personalized treatment from the coach. My daughter was not a number here. Of course, she was introduced to her student-athlete host and then met the other prospect that was on the visit. Much of her schedule was consistent with her previous experience. Based on AJ's excitement, I ended up catching a flight a bit later that day. Needless to say, I was also very impressed with the campus, the coach and the potential. From our vantage, this was really clouding the decision-making process.

That was our experience, but how did my daughter feel?

95

She agreed that the campus was great. She loved the coach and was impressed with the training program. However, she was uncertain about team fit. It wasn't that the students weren't nice. In fact, everything went according to plan, but my daughter just didn't feel that gel with this group of athletes. Make no mistake, this is an important consideration in making the final decision.

6 Surefire Ways to Know if the team fit is a No-Go

#1 Pay close attention to athlete-to-athlete and coach-to-athlete relationships. Does it seem strained? Is the coach too buddy buddy with athletes? Some things won't be said, but body language will do the talking. Team energy is an important part of the experience. Many of these relationships will become lifelong. Athletes need to feel confident in talking one on one with the coach, especially when it comes to getting feedback on your performances and your daily team interactions.

#2 Check out the coach-to-athlete ratio. How many coaches on the staff work directly with event training? If the coach-to-athlete ratio is too high, this could be detrimental to time they can dedicate to your success.

#3 Is there an event specific coach for your race? You want to ensure that you have the opportunity to continue developing and progressing at the collegiate level. However, it can pose a problem if your coach has no love for your event or technical knowledge in this area. Find out about their running history and don't be afraid to respectfully ask questions about their credentials.

#4 What is the progression of current athlete performances in your event? Are they improving each season? What is the training protocol? Many of these questions can be answered by accessing team profiles on TFRRS. Just saying, you need to be in an environment that focuses on your long-term development, and this would include working with your coach to set goals.

#5 Who are the members of the support team? Is there a separate weight training specialist, sports performance specialist, athletic trainer or does the coach handle it all? A jack of all trades coach may be sacrificing too much coaching time putting out fires on other matters.

#6 Does this coach inspire you? Seems like a difficult quality to assess early on, but it is essential in a good coach. You want to be led by someone who can not only motivate when times are great, but that is perceptive and compassionate enough to encourage when things go awry. In this case, they'll give you what you need, and despite the fact that it is tough, you'll do it anyway.

These are questions that only your Rockstar can answer. There is no right or wrong, just a matter of preference. However, they should feel comfortable with their answers before making a final decision.

After the Visit

Soon after you have completed the official visit, while everything is fresh in your mind, these are a few important tasks that will help your Rockstar make a positive impression and prepare for the upcoming decision:

- Send a thank you email to the coach - Keep It Simple

"Dear Coach X,

Thank you for allowing me to take a closer look at University X. I really enjoyed meeting you, spending time with the team, and touring the campus. The experience helped me to see what I can expect from college life as a Raider. I truly appreciate your time and that you are considering me for your 2019 track recruitment class.

Thanks again and I look forward to speaking with you again soon.

Respectfully,

Your Name"

- Jot down details from your visit that you thought were pluses and minuses. These are items that you will use later to compare one school to another

- Answer the question, "Would I attend this college if I wasn't an athlete?"

CHAPTER 18

STEP 7: NEGOTIATING THE DEAL: How to Maximize Your Scholarship Opportunity

*"In business as in life, you don't get what you deserve
you get what you negotiate."*
Chester L. Karass

Once the offer is extended, your Rockstar will need to make a very important decision. Before this can be done, it is essential to compare apples to apples. This is the time that the parent is in the driver's seat. You should already have a document showing the financial award package and overall costs of the university. Armed with this letter from various schools, you should be as detailed as possible in your comparison to ensure it becomes crystal clear which opportunity is truly the best for your Rockstar. When I say, "crystal clear", I am really saying which opportunity will require the least out of pocket expense from your student-athlete and family. If you see something that you don't like, appeal. Colleges will consider adjusting your financial aid package if you ask and can provide a valid reason or introduce new information.

Word of caution never use the word "negotiate" during this process. More appropriate words would be reconsider, revisit or make adjustments. Remember, the ultimate goal is to select a great school and to go to school for free (or as close to free as possible). So, you must not lose sight of this and get caught up in the bells and whistles of your choices. Assuming each option is desirable, it will ultimately come down to cost.

> **Tip:** Financial aid awards can be based on merit, academic potential, ethnicity, special financial circumstances, family legacy or need. It can be awarded in the form of grants, scholarships, work study and loans. Earning outside scholarships (from somewhere other than the university, like your credit union, sorority or a major corporation) can really help reduce college expenses.

While I don't recommend using the term "negotiate" that is exactly what you will need to do.

How do you negotiate?

- Realize that your leverage comes from your offers. You should have proof of two-way communication with no fewer than five coaches.

- Having offers from schools within the same conference can work in your favor. You can request that one school match another by showing the financial award package.

- You must have written proof of your offer/communication

- Renegotiate how money is applied to your Rockstar's account so that it is most beneficial for your family

- Don't be afraid to ask for what you want

- Don't sign anything until you are happy with the offer

This process simply requires open communication between you and your Rockstar's university of choice. If things don't look the way you want, contact the coach and let them know that they are your first choice, but another school has presented a better financial package. You never know what they can or will do until you ask. Again, it really helps the negotiation process if the school you are attempting to match is within their conference.

Tip: If you don't have a financial award package but want to get an idea of the possible expenses before speaking with a coach, you can check the financial calculator. Most schools provide access to this tool on their school website. It's free and simple to use.

CHAPTER 19

STEP 8: MAKING THE DECISION

*"It's not so hard to make decisions,
when you know what your values are."*
Walt Disney

The light at the end of the tunnel is near. Your Rockstar has finally reached the pinnacle point in the recruitment process. All the research, visits and phone calls have culminated into making what may be their first important decision on their future.

In my daughter's case, by the time she finished her official visits, her list had been narrowed down from her top five to three schools. Really, it was more like two because one of those top choices hadn't really maintained ongoing communication. At any rate, each option had stellar academics and she had a very positive feeling about the campus environments and opportunities in her major coursework. While there were similarities, she felt that the subtle differences could potentially change the entire college experience. Being in a position to make this decision was new and fairly nerve-wracking because she simply didn't want to have any regrets. She tossed around comparisons of weather, team practice schedules and each coach's recruitment effort (how interested they seemed in her). Despite her struggle, the clock was ticking, which forced us to set a final date for the decision to be made.

Surprisingly, on the day before decision making morning, my husband received a call from a coach whose school she had already dropped from the list. "I was just calling to see if she would be willing to delay her decision."

This can happen, particularly when your Rockstar is being considered, but not the top recruit for a program. Maybe the top recruit chose a different team, or room opened up due to no prospects in another event. Regardless, a new opportunity and decision was now laid before my daughter.

"What do you think?" my husband and I asked.

This was a highly rated academic school that presented an opportunity that could be life-changing. Even so, she did not budge in her decision date, and decided not to add them to the list if it meant she would have to wait. In fact, that night she had to make a very difficult call to let a coach know that she would not attend.

"Hello Coach ___, this is ___. How are you? I am calling to let you know that I have decided to choose School X. I really appreciate the time that you have taken with me and wish you luck in the upcoming season."

The conversation was short, but nonetheless challenging. She was truly exasperated after making the call but felt some consolation that the decision was not made lightly.

8am the next morning marked decision making time!

We all woke up anxious about the call, yet equally excited at the fact that this process was just about over. Being that it was a school day, the confirmation call was also short and to the point.

As simple as that, it was done. My daughter left my husband and me in the living room smiling ear to ear, as she headed to school.

Lo and behold! We couldn't believe what happened next.

No more than an hour later my husband receives a text message asking for if we were available to talk. It was from the other top choice that hadn't communicated in a while. This was a call my daughter had waited so long to receive. "I will support her application," is what the coach said.

My jaw dropped, as my husband vigorously texted my daughter the news. Was it too late to rescind the acceptance we wondered, and why did the coach wait so long? Before we could ponder much more, and without hesitation, she texted back, "It's too late. My decision is made."

Making the final decision can be a challenge for anyone, but once it is made, accept it. Don't waste time with what ifs or maybes. Let your word be your reputation and have integrity in this process.

Integrity after you commit

Life slows down a bit after signing, although ongoing senior year activities and expenses will fill the voids in any schedule.

As far as your Rockstar is concerned, they will need to continue to be who they said they are. What that means is that the coach may continue to monitor them. Even after signing, my daughter's coach continued checking her meet results to see how she was performing throughout her senior year. In fact, he sent her a congratulations text after she achieved a new PR at the state track and field championship.

Of course, grades will also have to stay on track. Remember in the beginning of the process when the coach requested a list of your Rockstar's senior year courses to ensure they were of appropriate academic rigor? At the end of senior year, the university will request the final grades in the form of a full high school transcript, which shouldn't deviate much from the previous copy.

Staying out of trouble is also important. You have been granted an opportunity to attend college for free or at least at a reduced rate, which puts you in a unique class of students. After all this work it would be foolish to risk losing this incredible opportunity due to avoidable poor decision making. Student-athletes must be wise in selecting friends, the places they go and the choices they make when they get there.

CHAPTER 20

WHAT'S NEXT...

Congratulations! You have now done what most track parents will wish they had done by the time senior year rolls around. Trust me, standing by watching other kids sitting at the "signing table" gets old very quickly when your kid has no idea where they'll end up next year.

But you on the other hand...

You are now armed with the tools to promote your track athlete like a Rockstar and soar from nada to bada-Boom in 30 days or less. What does that really mean. Simple. It means that no matter where they start, you can take control of this process and open doors for your child to be recruited by a school of their choice that best matches their athletic ability and receive money for it.

I hope I have helped give you the motivation to get started today and dispelled many of the myths that may have been holding you back.

Again, I recommend purchasing the companion workbook to keep yourself organized and take notes through this journey. And if you find yourself needing a little extra assistance, shoot me an email and we can discuss a few options that best meet your needs.

Best wishes for your Rockstar's future success!

FINAL THOUGHT

Everything in this book is part of a proven blueprint. By following this step-by-step system, you can jumpstart the track recruiting process that can get your child on a college coach's radar in 30 days or less. In fact, you can repeat it again and again for as many athletes as you choose to help.

It's just that simple.

You might be thinking, "so, all I have to do is create an athletic profile, attach it to an email and send it out to as many qualified coaches as possible?"

Yep, that's basically the gist of it.

This easily understandable outline is simple to learn and duplicate. Hopefully, you will use it today to connect with college coaches and get the recruitment ball rolling for your Rockstar athlete. It's a no brainer!

When you follow this strategy, you're taking matters into your own hands to get a response from college coaches, which can open doors to official visits, and put your Rockstar in the driver's seat to choose their best college match.

Your success may even spark questions from your athlete's teammates and their parents about how you did it. They'll look at you as the track recruiting guru.

Once you email your profile, sit back and watch the responses come in. If all goes well, messages will come from qualified coaches who can offer your Rockstar an opportunity to use their track and field skills to pay for college.

Your Rockstar may even be at the center of a recruitment battle!

You'll also use tools and strategies to identify the best match for your Rockstar's talent level, learn how to maximize their scholarship potential and how to make the final decision. There are countless ways you can attract the attention of college coaches!

On top of it all, these methods are virtually free to implement.

That's right, you can save thousands of dollars by taking charge of the recruitment process and promoting your athlete like a Rockstar. It only takes one step at a time. There's no reason you cannot start getting emails from targeted coaches today. Now is the time to take the first step!

Apply this system and you'll give your athlete the best chance of realizing their dream of paying for college as a track and field athlete. I hope you benefit from following this process and enjoyed reading this book. I wish your Rockstar athlete much success in their future endeavors!

From one track parent to another,

Cara Jackson

PS – Want more on this topic? If you're ready to get started with this program, but need a bit more guidance, I want to invite you to take a look at the Promote 'Em Like a Rockstar Workbook. This is a companion manual that takes you step-by-step through the tasks within this book, while providing templates and questionnaires to keep you on track. The workbook will help jumpstart the recruitment process for your track and field athlete, as you are motivated to take immediate and consistent action, so you can:

- Get on a coach's radar
- Keep them interested until the deal is sealed
- Select a school that is the best match for your Rockstar's abilities
- Negotiate a financial agreement that is most helpful for your family's circumstances
- And ultimately, take control of this process!

With memory jogging fill-in- the-blanks and streamlining techniques, your Rockstar will be on the road to recruitment in no time.

APPENDIX 1
ONLINE RECRUITMENT SITES

My take on online athletic recruitment sites is that as long as they are FREE, you should try them. These sites allow you to post your Rockstar's profile either publicly or for "coaches only" view as a means of garnering interest in your Rockstar. Coaches who are looking to fill a particular void on their team can access these sites to quickly review specific athletes who meet their needs. You may primarily hear from Christian colleges, Div. II, and Division III colleges. These schools do not have the same recruiting budget, and often access the names of and reach out to student-athletes through online recruitment tools. It's a simple way of opening doors to lesser known sports programs who undoubtedly need athletes too.

To get started, you will answer a series of questions related to your Rockstar's accomplishments to include their contact information, graduation year and, of course, their fastest posted times and distances for each of their events, to name a few. You also have an opportunity to post:

- Pictures of your Rockstar standing on the podium at a meet (for example)

- videos of them during an intense training session or in competition

- links to articles where your Rockstar is featured

- a blog or add tidbits of breaking news as they achieve new and exciting things.

You can be as creative as you want, but always be honest and accurate with your details.

Once you have entered the requested information, you can make the profile live. This means that others will be able to view and respond to your Rockstar's profile if they are interested.

Again, in most cases, your interest and communication on these sites will come from smaller, less popular schools of which you may have never heard. This is just how it is, but that doesn't mean they aren't viable options. There are some schools whose need is so great that they will come to you, but for programs who are in high demand, this passive method of self-promotion may not work in your favor. However, this tool can be used in more than one way.

The first is what I have just described, which again is a passive method of informing others that your Rockstar is out there. But as you know, waiting for someone to find your Rockstar amongst thousands of other posted athletes, on a site that requires membership, when you have no earthly idea if the coach of your favorite University is even associated with the site, is not an effective plan. Clearly, I would not have written this book, and you would not be reading it, if getting recruited was that simple.

The second method, which transforms this latent activity to proactively marketing your Rockstar, is to add this link to your direct communication with their Target List of colleges. Because the format of these sites allows you to present your Rockstar's profile in a systematic and organized way, with such detail and easy updates, it can be a great resource to present to coaches. Adding this link simply requires you to copy and paste the URL of the profile page into your emails. This will create a direct link for your desired coaches to follow your Rockstar's accomplishments and highlights.

FYI, my daughter and son used different free versions of athletic recruitment sites and both received tons of emails. In fact, some of the Division III schools were top academic schools. They did not, however, pursue any of these options.

APPENDIX 2
RECRUITING TIMETABLE

Track and field recruiting is a unique animal. In addition to all the different events, from field to running, the recruiting methods and timeline for various track athletes shakes things up a bit too.

One huge factor that separates track from most other sports is the recruiting timetable. You may have noticed yourself that team sports seem to begin the recruitment process earlier than an individual sport, like track and field. It's okay, it just means that while some soccer and volleyball players begin receiving communication as they enter 9th grade (maybe even middle school for a select few), most track athletes won't hear much until their senior year. I've laid out a simple timetable of what you should follow to make this process a success:

9th Grade
- Focus on earning high grades and check your progress regularly (repeat 10th & 11th grades)
- Have fun competing in track and field (repeat 10th & 11th grades)
- Consider participating in summer track or a track camp/clinic (repeat 10th & 11th grades)
- Begin taking unofficial visits to local

116

college campuses (repeat 10th & 11th grades)

- Parents should video track performances and upload to YouTube (repeat 10th & 11th grades)

- Check your national ranking using Milesplit (repeat 10th & 11th grades)

10th Grade

- Begin fostering a relationship with your high school counselor and discuss your plans.

- Take the PSAT/PLAN to gauge your potential on the SAT and ACT

- Review the NCAA core course requirements

- Begin taking unofficial visits to college campuses in other states

- Start creating your Target List of colleges

- Register with NCAA & NAIA eligibility Centers

11th Grade

- Meet with your high school counselor to ensure your class schedule meets the NCAA core course requirements

- Begin sending highlight announcements to coaches

- Continue making unofficial visits to Target

117

List of colleges

- Take SAT/ACT Tests (retake as often as needed)

- Consider a SAT Test Prep class or private tutor

- Use TFRRS to assess where hidden opportunities may exist

12th Grade

- Begin emailing your cover letter and Athletic Profile to let coaches know of your interest level

- Follow up on any responses from college coaches

- Make official visits to your top 5 school choices

- Notify coaches if you are no longer interested

- Complete college application (Common App)

- Commit to compete in track and field at the school of your choice!

APPENDIX 3
UNDERSTANDING THE ATHLETIC RECRUITING CALENDAR

There are other important dates that you should know as it relates to the recruiting process. These dates indicate such times as when and how a coach can communicate with prospective athletes. Due to the exact date ranges varying from year to year, and delicate nature of this topic, it is best that you check with the NCAA Guide for College Bound Student Athletes for the specific details.

NCAA.org or call (800) 638-3731

The terms that you will need to be aware of and that describe these periods in the recruitment process are contact, evaluation, and dead.

Contact Period: Contact describes any face-to-face meeting between prospect and coach or anyone representing the college-bound student athlete beyond "hello." This period is the most open for coaches to interact with, visit and observe prospects. During the contact period, the coach can conduct home visits.

Evaluation: Coaches can visit prospects at their school or at any off-campus location to observe them train. This gives coaches a chance to assess the prospects athletic ability in person. During this period, coaches cannot conduct home visits.

Dead Period: This is the most restricted in the recruitment process. A coach cannot have any off-campus interaction, evaluation or meetings with a prospect, and they cannot come to see an athlete compete. If a prospect happens to be on campus, no in person contact is allowed.

Letter of Intent (LOI): this is a signed contract between the recruited student-athlete and the university which acknowledges the agreed upon terms of the athletic scholarship and commits the athlete to that institution.

APPENDIX 4
SIGNING DAY

The day of reckoning has arrived!

Signing Day is a day of celebration for many student-athletes. In front of their peers and their school's athletic staff, recruited athletes sit down at a table in the middle of the school's media center or gymnasium, wearing the t-shirt or cap of their future university. Typically, with their parents or coaches seated on either side of them, these athletes formally sign their National Letter of Intent (NLI).

The NLI is a legal contract and financial agreement binding the terms that have been established between the student-athlete and the university.

All sports have specific dates when NLIs can be signed, which include an early period and regular signing period. For track, the early signing period is around the second week of November. The regular period is the following April-August.

There are some additional points that you should be award of:

- Student-athletes are not required to sign an NLI. It is completely voluntary, but in most cases, works in the athlete's favor.

- This contract is between the school and the university, not the student-athlete and coach.

- There are penalties for breaking this contract.

Although the process only takes seconds, many people choose to make a big deal out of this day. They'll invite teachers, family members and as many students as the facility can hold. Oftentimes, coaches will say a few encouraging words about the athlete prior to penning their signature, and in some cases, parents will also speak. Afterwards, cake or cookies are made available to the guests. It's a fun and exciting time for student-athletes and should be a memorable event.

APPENDIX 5
IVY RECRUITMENT

If your athlete's academic profile is strong enough, athletic recruitment to an Ivy League school may be an option.

As previously mentioned, these institutions do not offer scholarships. However, due to their substantial endowments, Ivy League universities are typically able to provide funding to athletes in the form of grants. These grants may cover more than 90% of the student's college expenses, depending on the family's income and other factors affecting their financial status. In some cases, it may cost less to attend Harvard or Columbia than your state university.

Ivy League schools are recognized as some of the top universities in the world, and they are certainly worth considering if your Rockstar has consistently performed well in the classroom and on standardized tests. If Ivy recruitment seems like a possibility, there are few differences between Ivies and other schools that you should know.

Ivies use a unique formula to determine eligibility of a prospective student-athlete. Although certain elements vary based on the institution, generally, a student with a 3.7 unweighted gpa and a composite score of at least 30 on the ACT (for example) would be a potential candidate for Ivy League recruitment. It is not a guarantee, but an athlete at this level should attempt admission through the athletic route.

Understand that this simply gives you a basic idea of who may qualify, but there are other factors and calculations that each school will use to make their decision.

In fact, a formula known as the Academic Index (AI) is a tool that coaches use to determine if a prospect is recruitable. It is basically a calculation that creates a ranking for a student-athlete based on their gpa and test scores. The resultant number must fall within a certain standard deviation of the AI scores of non-student athletes. For sports such as football and basketball, which are typically priority sports, these universities may be a bit more lenient on the AI scores as compared to track and field athletes.

Another major difference is that Ivy League schools do not issue a "Letter of Intent" or have a signing day. Instead, they use what is called a "Likely Letter." This letter is an unofficial offer that serves as a written commitment between the student and university that is sent from the Admissions office prior to the actual admissions date. Athletes and non-athletes who are coveted recruits can both receive a Likely Letter.

In terms of the signing day, some student-athletes will host a "fake signing." They will wear their shirt, sit at a table and announce the institution that they will attend and compete, without actually signing any documents. It gives them an opportunity to be publicly recognized and celebrated by their peers and the school athletic department, just like other recruited athletes.

The last point that I will make as it relates to Ivy recruitment is that they typically want athletes to make a firm decision before November 1st. In most cases, Ivy League schools would like to complete their athletic recruitment and have their recruited athletes commit as early-decision admits. While this is not a requirement, it is the preferred method for many Ivy coaches. So, if this is a route that your Rockstar may take, be prepared to make an early decision if the opportunity presents.

APPENDIX 6
MEETS THAT CAN MAKE A DIFFERENCE
TO COLLEGE COACHES

Not all meets are equal. What I mean by that is there are a few different track and field meets that are more valuable to college coaches than others. Many of these meets are hosted across the nation and any athlete who is serious about running in college should strive to compete in at least one of them. In most cases, athletes have to qualify by running a specified time or throwing and jumping a certain distance to be eligible. College coaches attend these meets and commonly check the results. Competing and performing well can open doors for your Rockstar.

Here are a few examples of track and field meets to keep on your radar:
- State Championship Meet (in your home state)
- New Balance Nationals (XC and Track)
- USATF Junior Olympics
- AAU Junior Olympics
- Disney/ESPN Wide World of Sports AAU Track & Field Championship
- Golden South
- Brooks PR (invite only)

You can google any of these meet names and the current year to find out when it will be hosted and what is required to participate. In fact, most of these events are listed on the Milesplit or CoachO websites. Remember, even if your athlete does not qualify to participate in any of these meets they can still be recruited.

APPENDIX 7
CHECKLIST ON DIFFERENCES BETWEEN HIGH SCHOOL AND COLLEGE TRACK

College Track Athletes should be prepared for:

✓ **Running Indoor and Outdoor Track**
New recruits should be prepared to begin training in the fall with indoor meets beginning in late November, early December. Gone are the days of waiting until after Christmas break to get track ready.

✓ **Weight Training**
Most collegiate track and field programs require at least 2 days of weight training. Many high school athletes never touch weights.

✓ **Split practices**
High school athletes typically begin practice shortly after the school day ends. The entire team will meet on the track and separate by event. Well, in college some athletes who compete in the same event may practice at different times. There's a chance sprinters may never see distance runners train.

✓ **Other Goodies that Student-Athletes can Enjoy**
It's not all running, jumping and throwing like high school. Some days athletes may have cross training, like yoga or swimming. Most have access to world class facilities, trainers

and sports specialists. You'll even get a per diem to buy food at meets.

APPENDIX 8
WHAT TO KNOW ABOUT INDOOR TRACK MEETS

Everyone focuses on outdoor track meets, but indoor meets are also valuable. Depending on where you live, especially for those in the southern and western states, participating in indoor track meets in high school may not be very common.

These meets are typically hosted at indoor facilities, which are much smaller venues than the standard track stadium. In fact, with the indoor tracks being 200m, some events require 2-3 times as many cycles to reach the distance of a standard outdoor track, plus the athlete has to negotiate sharper turns. There are even a few events that cannot be performed during the indoor season, like the 400m hurdles or discus, simply due to space limitations. Competing in indoor track during high school does allow athletes to show another aspect of their athleticism. Events are shorter, thus requiring more speed, which can give recruiting coaches a different perspective on your Rockstar's abilities.

It is also important to understand that in college, track and field athletes compete in both indoor and outdoor seasons. While many athletes participate in different events during the indoor season, anyone considering being a part of a collegiate track and field program should be prepared for this. There is even a separate championship meet at the conference and national level for indoor track.

APPENDIX 9:
COLLEGE TRACK EVENTS FOR INDOOR COMPETITIONS

There are fewer indoor than outdoor track events and many of the distances are reduced due to space limitations.

Running Events:
Sprint events
- 60-meter dash
- 200-meter dash
- 400-meter dash

Distance events
- 500-meter run (rare)
- 800-meter run
- Mile run
- 3,000-meter run
- 5,000-meter run

Hurdle Events
- 60-meter hurdles

Relay events
- 1,600-meter relay
- Distance medley relay

Field events:
Jumping events
- High jump
- Pole vault
- Long jump
- Triple jump

Throwing events
- Shot put
- Weight throw

Multi-events

Heptathlon

APPENDIX 10:
STAYING HEALTHY AS A TRACK ATHLETE

Knee pain & stiff joints & foot aches, oh my!

I can vividly remember track athletes sporting white tape double wrapped under foot arches, traveling up and around the shins, reminiscent of standing wraps on the legs of derby horses.

Back in my high school running days, this was a common occurrence. The purpose was to alleviate pressure and protect the ligaments and tendons while the athletes were in competition. These run-of-the-mill injuries seemed unavoidable and we learned to just run with the pain until we couldn't.

Today it's not nearly as common.

Because that was before athletes realized that there are ways to stay healthy and optimize performance.

You guessed it, athletes are maximizing their potential through chiropractic.

It's true, runners need chiropractic.

Why, you ask?

For starters, the:

• Constant pounding on pavement during long runs on cement around the high school campus creates micro-traumas to a runner's joints.

• Quick bursts of sprinting after insufficiently warming up the hamstrings can lead to muscle tears, strains and painful spasms that hinder performance and completely pull athletes out of competition.

• Deep and throbbing lower back pain often caused by overworking abdominal muscles compounded by underworking back extensors can put runners in the stands instead of the on the starting line.

• Increasing mileage without proper progression can result in excruciating pain on the bottom of the foot that literally stops runners in their tracks.

Even the Olympic Gold Medalist and Decathlete, Dan O'Brian confirmed, "Chiropractic is essential for running. If I could put a percentage value on it I would say that I compete 8-10% better from regular chiropractic care."

If you've never been, you're probably wondering what chiropractors actually do and how does it help runners?

Simple!   -Pain relief, injury prevention, increased mobility, and enhanced recovery.

The chiropractic adjustment does the trick!

Most procedures are done by hand, they are non-invasive, and many people say they just "feel good."

If you want to join other athletes in getting the edge in competition and perform at your optimal potential, choose chiropractic to get you better faster.

Atlanta Sports & Injury Center for Rehab

APPENDIX 11
RESOURCES TO HELP YOU

Disclosure: Some of the links below are affiliate links, meaning at no additional cost to you, I will earn a commission should you choose to click through and make a purchase.

If making a purchase, please use my name in the referral prompt: **"Cara Jackson"**

SAT and ACT Prep Service ....Prepscholars.com

Summer Track Entity...............................Aau.com

Summer Track Entity...............................Usatf.com

High School Track Meet Calendars ...Milesplit.com

Indoor and summer meet calendars ....CoachO.com

Hurdles Training ....sprint hurdles

Throws Club Throw1Deep.org

Pole Vault Atlanta ....pvatl.com

High Jump Training...................kangaroo track club

Training Programs & Equipment Sites:

Complete Track and Field Training...................CTF

Track Equipment....Complete Track and Field Store

ABOUT THE AUTHOR

 After documenting her daughter's athletic recruitment process to a Division I university, and successfully using the same method to promote her son, Cara Jackson has created this essential guidebook. Transforming your role from parent to promoter, it will empower you to apply the same tools that she used to navigate track recruitment for your athlete.

The format is simple. The plan is proven.

Join Cara on this journey and accelerate the path from diddly to done in the track recruitment game!

Cara is a former high school athlete, summer track coach, and the parent of college track and field athletes (four USATF youth All-Americans). Her unique perspective after serving more than twenty years in different roles in the sport makes reading this book a no-brainer for track parents who want to open doors, access a great education, and save money for their student-athlete.

Professionally, she and her husband are Doctors of Chiropractic, and operate Atlanta Sports & Injury Center for Rehab.

Cara enjoys uncovering wonderfully inexpensive life-changing opportunities for her kids and creating memorable experiences for her family.

Made in the USA
Monee, IL
29 April 2021